# I Don't Believe It!
## Christopher Lane

*Another look at some of the tricky bits
of the Bible*

*with Questions for Group or Individual use*

GW00372014

## Foreword by Russ Parker
## Illustrations by Lynn New

Published by Chrysolite Publishing

First published July 2012 by Chrysolite Publishing, Carisbrooke,
Isle of Wight.
Copyright © 2012 Christopher Lane

ISBN: 978-0-9572906-0-0

Also by the Author    The Holy Caterpillar 2006

Illustrations © 2012 by Lynn New

Typesetting by stephendarlington.co.uk

Printed on the Isle of Wight by Biltmore Printers, Newport

# I Don't Believe It!

## CONTENTS

# ACKNOWLEDGEMENTS AND THANKS

Revd Dr Russ Parker is an Anglican priest who had held the post of Director of the Acorn Christian Healing Foundation since 1995. Author of several Christian books including 'Healing Dreams', 'Free to Fail', 'Healing Death's Wounds' (with Michael Mitton), 'Forgiveness is Healing', 'Healing Wounded History', 'Listening, Healing and Reconciliation', 'Wild Spirit' and 'Dream Stories'.

Among his many appointments, Russ is both a Patron of Carisbrooke Priory and leader of The Fellowship of Christ the Healer

Lynn New has followed a successful career as poet, author and illustrator for nearly twenty years. Based on the Isle of Wight, her work is known and appreciated across the country. Her latest book 'The Child Within' is a beautiful and perceptive account of her childhood years, which were marked by prolonged illness.

The author is also very thankful for all who have helped in the conception and production of this book, among them Steve Darlington for preparing the copy for printing and Rob & Tim Lane who have carefully checked the drafts and dared to suggest the corrections that Dad might make!

*To my wife Ann
for so often being a patient Margaret
to my occasional Victor*

# FOREWORD BY RUSS PARKER

Every now and then a book comes our way which has a freshness and a challenge to look at familiar subjects and give you a sudden, new insight which will make you hungry to go back to the Scriptures and look for more. Chris Lane's "I Don't Believe it" is one of those books. Be prepared to be opened to new possibilities and to have some of your well worn assumptions overturned. Chris writes with a refreshing honesty about his own wrestling with troublesome texts and ends up all the richer for doing so. He writes in a clear and simple way which draws you in to his heart and his love of scripture. Jesus steps out of the pages of the Bible and is dynamically present again. This is a wonderful book! He includes some of his own poetry which I have greatly enjoyed down the years and the questions at the end of each chapter are not dull or bland but invite you to a place of engaging with this marvellous Christ who will not be tied to our horizons.

Chris was for many years the Chaplain of Carisbrooke Priory, a Christian Healing centre on the Isle of Wight and hence his book is threaded through with his years of coming alongside the most broken of people and being Jesus for their need. It has been a very costly road that he has walked but one which he was glad and willing to walk. His teaching helps us to connect with this vibrant Christ who calls us to be his name and heart for those who need to be honoured into regaining their full humanity and grace in God.

So hold on to your hats because you are in for a stimulating ride when you open the pages of this book.

Rev. Dr. Russ Parker
Director
Acorn Christian Healing Foundation

# FOREWORD BY THE AUTHOR

I'd been in Southampton General for a week and now was the day they were to deliver the diagnosis. I lay on the bed, my wife Ann sitting on a chair alongside, neither of us having any idea of what was about to come; "We're sorry to tell you, but the clinical diagnosis is Motor Neurone Disease."

You'd be forgiven for thinking that may have had something to do with the title of this book. In fact it came to mind more than a year before that memorable date, 22nd November 2011. During my ministry I found myself often preaching on bits of the Bible that had a habit of evoking just such a thought deep inside, if I dared admit it. Don't get me wrong. I am not a confirmed unbeliever. Quite the reverse.

I could write a book about how much God has done in my life, revealing his amazing love and power. In fact, thinking about it I already have. 'The Holy Caterpillar' (2006) was prompted by being called to change beliefs you'd always assumed were unchangeable. And for me personally that often uncomfortable journey was made all the more bearable and even liberating by extraordinary and repeated assurances of His presence.

Being a fan of *'One Foot in the Grave'*, a popular TV comedy from the nineties, I've always had a lot of sympathy for poor old Victor Meldrew. His exasperated outburst was, I feel, born out of an underlying belief in the rightness and goodness of things. And when events so often transpired to blow that belief out of the water, you couldn't help but feel sorry for the old misery, to say nothing of his long-suffering wife.

So this book is necessarily quite personal. It's about seeking to hold firm to belief in a God of perfect love and justice, when some of what the Christian faith has traditionally taught may seem to say the opposite. I suspect there are many people out there who have been simply unable to believe, due to what has been presented to them. Others of us may live a life of faith but with part of our mind closed off, choosing to disregard the tricky bits.

I write as one with what they call 'a high view of Scripture'. I've never been comfortable with the idea of treating the Bible as any other historical document. For me it is the inspired Word of God and that same Holy Spirit who inspired its writing, can and should be expected to interpret it to each new generation. In the Christian faith there have long been three main approaches to interpreting Scripture.

The first holds the Bible itself to be the final arbiter of truth, the second sees the application of human reason as being at least as vital, the third recognises the Church as the source of wisdom, drawing on its teaching both old and new. Basically these give rise to the three 'parties' of evangelical, liberal and catholic. If I'm pushed (and I confess I don't particularly like being pushed) I hold most comfortably to the first position. But then again my heart cries out that there must be a place for reason. Reason is after all part of what God has given us, part of his image in which he has created us. And then again who am I to disregard the teaching of others far wiser than me that have gone before, unless with very good reason? Jesus speaks of the wise teacher who brings out of his storehouse treasures old and new. Some things must clearly be held on to at all costs, such as Jesus' uncompromising command: *"Love your enemies, do good to those who hate you, bless those who curse you." (Luke 6:27)* Others now lost or overlooked, need rediscovering.

At the end of the day, literally, I want to be able to sleep peacefully in my bed, confident I really can trust in the Lord of all the earth to do right. I am always inspired by those words from the Song of Moses;

*"I will proclaim the Name of the Lord*
*Oh praise the greatness of our God!*
*He is the Rock, his works are perfect*
*and all his ways are just.*
*A faithful God who does no wrong,*
*upright and just is He."*
*(Deut: 32 3-4)*

Another great figure from the Old Testament was Job. After all that happened to him, if anyone was justified in 'doing a Victor Meldrew' it was Job. But even he found a way to still believe in the goodness of God. I do hope and pray what I offer may, with his grace, help you do the same.

Finally a word or two about how you might like to use this book. Each chapter is based on a passage of the Bible. In some cases it is included in full, in others I have given just the reference. I do encourage you to read each passage through first. I recognise the great responsibility of interpreting Scripture, what it refers to itself as *'handling holy things'*. The Holy Spirit may well have something to say to you through these passages that I have not included and let's be honest, he may even have something different to say!

Each chapter concludes with a set of questions. You may find these useful in thinking around what has been written, either on your own or in a group. As one who has a dislike of examinations and questionnaires I would quite understand if you'd rather give them a miss.

Also included are some poems, mostly written a number of years ago. There's something about poetry that is good for helping the imagination to explore, and this I have often found valuable when wrestling with aspects of faith that are not cut and dried. Sometimes it's just fun playing with words! I hope you enjoy them.

Chris Lane
Carisbrooke
May 2012

# EVENING PRAYER BEFORE AN OPEN BIBLE

In the deepening evening still
shadows of gloom,
alone with a light
in a candle lit room,
thoughts and love feelings
now eddy together,
come swimming in circles
from here to forever.

Grasp out for anchorage
cling to a line,
focus on pin points of light
as they shine
out of black and white pages,
like cats' eyes ascend;
two open held palms
of my Carpenter Friend.

# CHAPTER ONE
# THE BROAD WAY AND THE NARROW WAY

*"Enter through the narrow gate. For wide is the gate and broad is the road that leads to destruction, and many enter through it. But small is the gate and narrow the road that leads to life, and only a few find it." Matt 7:13-14*

In at the deep end! Of all the bits that have bothered me, this has to be up with there with the best of them. And the cause of my disquiet I never heard put so clearly as when, a few years ago, we were listening to a preacher expound on it, aided by two drawings. The first was of the broad road, busy with all kinds of people. There was a couple walking arm in arm looking lovingly at each other, a young mum pushing a buggy, an elderly woman with a stick and yes, a couple of lads swigging from cans. Everyone looked cheerful enough, though blissfully unaware they were heading for the chasm in front of them, out of which licked tongues of fire.

Picture two was of a narrow winding path with just one person on it. There was no one else in front or behind him and certainly no one beside him, the path wasn't wide enough! He was a young man, walking alone and quite frankly with an expression somewhere between blankness and misery. The message simply reinforced the wretched pictures which spoke more than a thousand regrettable words. At the end of the service, apart from feeling sick inside, my wife and I spent a considerable time talking to and praying with a middle aged man who had been sitting beside us and was now sobbing deeply. Some might say, that's a small price to pay for the salvation of his soul. No omelettes without breaking eggs. He might be in tears now but how much worse would he feel burning for eternity in hell? As it happened his tears were far less for himself than for all the members of his family and friends who as far as he could see ticked none of the right boxes to qualify them for a place on the narrow path. In my more rebellious moments I have tried to picture the chaos were everyone to transfer at the same time from the broad to the narrow path. And what of those who want to travel in pairs, as a family, as a community? The truth is my problem is more with the pictures than the parable, which perhaps underlines the huge responsibility anyone has who is called to teach or preach.

Let's just stay with those pictures a little longer and allow me to turn to the One who first gave us the parable that inspired this particular interpretation of it.

*Lord Jesus, I really believe you to be the perfect embodiment of wisdom and love. So help me please to see that in these words of yours. Are you really saying that the vast majority of humanity will burn in hell? Is heaven to be populated by a tiny exclusive bunch of individuals who kept themselves hermetically isolated from this wicked world, for fear of being tempted by it? Is hell to be overflowing with millions upon millions of tormented souls? People who are otherwise basically good at heart, people born into another religion and those who never heard the Gospel, people who rejected faith through being fed a distorted version of it or through being abused by a Church leader?*

Over the years, each time I've come back to this troubling text I've felt in my bones there must be another interpretation. The first chink of light came as I considered the ancient door leading into the Close where my Theological College was situated in Salisbury. It had what in Jesus' day would have been described as a 'flea', a small narrow doorway set within one of two large gates. You had no chance of getting through this 'flea' in your 4 x 4, it was even a struggle loaded up with bags of shopping.

So it says something about travelling light, avoiding the kind of devotion to 'things' that can ultimately rob us of life. But what if this was not two separate roads, but two separate ways of travelling along the same road? Time and again as we go through life the choice is ours with every decision we take. Will it be the broad or the narrow way? Will we make our choices according to the principles and values of the kingdom of this world or the Kingdom of Heaven? One way each decision leads to destruction, the other to life.

This brings me to my second chink. As I see it, there is one crucial word in all this. It is what Jesus says the broad way will lead to. The word is translated as *'destruction'* in most versions, *'perdition'* in some, and in just one as far as I'm aware as *'hell'*. I'm not a Greek scholar, so I tend to go for the word most versions choose, especially the more modern ones, though interestingly the dear old King James has it as *'destruction'*. To my mind there's all the difference in the world between *'destruction'* and *'hell'*. Perdition or hell is defined by the Oxford Dictionary as damnation, which in turn is defined as eternal punishment in hell. Now hell is destruction but destruction is not necessarily hell, just as the loss of a loved one is bereavement but bereavement is not necessarily the loss of a loved one. The loss of anything dear to you can be a bereavement; a job, a house, a pet, a limb, your mobility.

So what do I believe Jesus is saying? I'm getting there but first to reiterate my faith in him as the Lord of love and mercy as well as truth and as such he only speaks words that embody all of these. And his words are not intended as a dire threat. Sadly, far too much preaching in the past and even to the present day relies on terrifying people into faith, majoring on the dire consequences of not unquestioningly accepting what is being said.

I have a real problem with medieval doom paintings, those huge murals that used to cover many a church wall, with numerous naked figures writhing in pain tormented by an army of demons. They were often on the Chancel arch where the congregation had little chance of not allowing their eyes to dwell on the images, especially when the sermon was dull or the liturgy incomprehensible. They were like those wretched unavoidable flat screen TV's you find in pubs. Why for heaven's sake did they always have to be pictures of hell? Why not some inspiring depiction of creation or one of the scenes from Jesus' life? And I'm sure it's no accident these paintings were one of the few occasions when the Church permitted the depiction of human nakedness. Another reason to find it hard to keep your eyes off them! But the effect it was intended to have was from childhood upwards you were to associate nakedness with evil and eternal punishment. How much psychological damage has that bit of teaching been responsible for? And what of the effect these images have on all those children in church and others with impressionable minds? It would be interesting to see the reaction these days if some over zealous primary school teacher thought such a scene would make a nice wall display. I actually suspect Oliver Cromwell did God a service in covering many of them over with whitewash, though now of course in the interest of history there are those who would have them painstakingly restored. If we must have them, perhaps they should come with a health warning; *'This image may seriously damage your faith in a God of love and mercy'!* But come on Victor, enough of your rant and back to the text.

What I do believe my Jesus is saying is this. As we travel through life we will need to continually make choices both big and small and decide which of two ways to take, according to the values of the world's kingdom or his. Consider first the major decisions of life and for a moment let's revisit one of his other parables, The Wise and Foolish Builders.

***"Therefore everyone who hears these words of mine and puts them into practice is like a wise man who built his house upon the rock. The rain came down, the streams rose***

*and the winds blew and beat upon that house; yet it did not fall, because it had its foundations on the rock. But everyone who hears these words of mine and does not put them into practice is like a foolish man who built his house on sand. The rain came down, the streams rose and the winds blew and beat against that house and it fell with a great crash."*
*Matt 7:24-27*

If we build all our hopes and dreams on anything less than God we will ultimately suffer disappointment, loss and destruction. It's not a threat but simply a statement of fact made by a loving Father to his vulnerable child. If everything that matters most to us is invested in a human relationship or acquiring a skill or certain level of education, a vocation or anything else in this life, we shall experience great destruction, as when the house on the sand succumbed to the storm. This is the broad way that will lead to destruction, because all these things, like ourselves are temporal and subject to accident, sickness and ultimately death. Of course, many of these aspirations are perfectly noble and there's no reason not to desire them and pursue them. But they must be seen and held in perspective, in the light of our greatest desire, which is to be our eternal relationship with God. This principle does not only apply to these big issues of life but as much to the everyday, simple things.

Take the weather for example. In our climate the weather is guaranteed to challenge us on a regular basis. To say we can do nothing about it is wrong. We may not be able to change it, but we do have a choice of two ways in which to react to it. If every time it rains we take the easy and broad way and mutter and grumble about 'this filthy weather', we will talk ourselves into a frame of mind that destroys our peace. Apart from anything else, rain is not filthy and without it we all suffer from drought and will ultimately die. And if we insist on voicing our negative thoughts publicly, we'll take others down with us. I love the fact that those living in the Western Isles and Ireland, who see far more rain than sunshine describe such weather as *'soft'*. I imagine over the generations those who were unable to accept and even enjoy wet weather have probably long since died out due to the evolutionary principle of selection pressure! The weather may seem quite trivial but I suspect if we habitually react negatively, that is, destructively to it we will react similarly to every knock, set back and trial that life sends.

I also suspect as we reflect on our lives in eternity, we'll be shown just how many 'broad way' decisions we made, often without even realising it. The broad way is among other things the line of least resistance, going with the flow. The narrow way on the other hand compels us to slow down and take care, like those bollards in the road for calming the traffic. Sometimes we may have been just too busy, too distracted, too anxious to notice the narrow way we were being invited to take, such as a word of kindness or encouragement. And how often have we snapped at someone because we are so wound up? That is a broad way decision to not curb the tongue and it is destructive. Not necessarily disastrous, not all destruction is, but destructive it is of good and peaceful relationships. Much is repairable with an honest word of apology. And Jesus is all about restoration, which is the antidote to destruction. He and his Father are in the business of restoring what the Enemy wants to destroy and in this simple teaching Jesus is telling us how to do it.

So to sum up thus far. Taking everything else Scripture says, not least how it is God's will that everyone shall be saved, I have to say I reject the traditional interpretation that in this parable Jesus is saying all but a handful are going to hell. Rather I believe what he is offering us are words of life. He is saying that we repeatedly have the choice to live our lives in a way that is either life enhancing or life destroying. The choice is ours and is to be made daily on the road as we travel. Each choice will be determined by what we consider our greatest treasure to be and whether we hold our relationship with God more precious than anything else. And that relationship should govern how we react to disappointments, such as when events or other people let us down or fail to meet our expectations. Bear in mind how often we may do the same to them.

I said in the Foreword I had a certain sympathy for Victor Meldrew. In truth of course his exasperation will, in the end, probably do nothing to prevent it happening again and all the while both he and his wife and everyone around him are robbed of peace. His way is I'm afraid an example of the broad way. The narrow way, as Jesus not only teaches but lives out, is to meet those who let him down with understanding, mercy and compassion. The greater the wrongdoing, the harder it may be to shed enough of our pride to squeeze through the narrow gate. But he has gone before us and shown us it can be done, probably not in our own strength but certainly with his.

*When passing through the gates of pearly splendour,*
*Victors, we rest with Thee, through endless days.*

('We rest on Thee' Edith Gilling Cherry d.1897)


POSTSCRIPT

Do I hear someone ask; *'So don't you believe there is a hell?'* As Churchill would say *'Oh yes!'* You only have to pick up a paper or watch the news to see the latest example of mankind choosing the broad way of destruction at the expense of so much life. And just as we can have a foretaste of heaven on earth so the opposite is true. But as to who will ultimately be consigned to that place of eternal loss, I hold on to certain Biblical truths. In the last book of the Bible, Jesus' revelation from Glory to his special friend John, he makes it clear (Rev 20:10) it will be very largely for Satan and those other fallen angels who have totally rejected God. It could be construed there are some mortals who at the very last choose to throw in their lot with them rather than with God. It could also be construed that it is only to be Satan and the other fallen angels, the beast and the false prophet who will be tormented for ever.

The terrible disasters described in Revelation that God visits on the earth in the last days are only allowed because there is by then no alternative and his longing is that even at this last hour some who have resolutely rejected him thus far may yet turn and be saved. And at the end of the last day, there is only one person given the responsibility of saying where we are each to go. Not us and certainly not the preacher! And that person is the Lord Jesus Christ, Judge of all. In my heart I truly believe, hope and pray there will be very few of us in that awful place. But as the decision is to be made by the God of love and mercy, I do believe we have nothing to fear. So sleep well!

And when we wake, let's discover we can really live this life so much better by asking Jesus to help us throughout each day. He has left us the Holy Spirit that we may recognise and avoid the choices that will lead to destruction and seek and embrace those that will lead to life.

QUESTIONS

1. How have you always interpreted this parable?

2. What 'broad way' decisions do you think we might make without realising it?

3. Can you think of a 'narrow way' decision that was especially difficult to make?

4. What do you think are the characteristics of the life Jesus says we shall find through choosing the narrow way?

5. If you ever told anyone to 'go to hell', did you really hope they would, did you believe they would?

POEM

In choosing a poem to conclude this chapter, I've come up with one that is a personal confession of a 'broad way' decision. It dates back to the early eighties when I was still working for Bromley Council in South London. My discipleship recently restored, I had joined the Christian Union and was due to go to a lunchtime meeting but first had to dash into the supermarket to grab a sandwich. In front of me at the checkout was an old lady, struggling with her shopping and keeping us all waiting.

## CHECKOUT

Before me in the queue
stands a short and grey haired figure,
anonymous old woman,
open purse in shaky hand;
pathetically fumbling
with stubborn crooked fingers,
she hears with pain the grumbling
from the women close behind.

My mind is idly drifting
and the promises I made
on my knees that very morning
now evaporate away;
as there with all the others
I am busily deriding
the plight of this old woman
and her deepening dismay.

Aggravating hindrance
irritating long delay
time wasting and annoying
stupid woman in my way-
Jesus, look at her!

Yes, look at her now
with the vision of Jesus,
look at this woman
through his caring eyes;
the woman before you,
the daughter he sees is
a widow of one
and a mother of two,
who cries in the morning
for the ones she once knew.

There's Harry her eldest,
ten years now in Christchurch
with wife and three children
she'll never be meeting;
one phone call each Christmas
sends dutiful greeting,
saying they missed her;
love is dear
at long distance.

And the youngest is not far away,
pressed into his flying jacket
deep within the clay
beneath a peaceful Kentish field.

# CHAPTER TWO
# THE PARABLE OF THE SOWER

*"A farmer went out to sow his seed. As he was scattering the seed some fell along the path, and the birds came and ate it up. Some fell on rocky places, where it did not have much soil. It sprang up quickly, because the soil was shallow. But when the sun came up the plants were scorched, and they withered because they had no root. Other seed fell among thorns, which grew up and choked the plants. Still other seed fell on good soil, where it produced a crop - a hundred, sixty or thirty times what was sown. He who has ears let him hear." Matt 13: 3-9*

My problems with this one crept up on me over the years. As a child I had no difficulty, or so I thought, in understanding exactly what Jesus was saying. Much of the Bible was impenetrable to me but not this bit. From an early age I loved gardening and all things of nature. I knew the thrill of sowing seeds and waiting for them to grow and the pitfalls that awaited them including birds, weeds and drought. All I thought was missing were the slugs and snails. Perhaps God had banished them from the Holy Land, in which case it seemed most of them had sought refuge in our garden!

As with any story you cannot help but identify with one of the characters. In this case I began to wonder what kind of seed I was. Maybe a sermon at Evensong encouraged me to apply the parable to my own life. To my shame, I never had any doubt that of course I was one of the good soils. But as with school, I had learnt the best place to be was in the middle of class. Those at the bottom were always in fear of being put down into the lower stream. Those at the top were always expected by the teacher to know the answer and set a good example, whilst at the same time being looked on with suspicion by your peers. As with any herd of animals, the safest place is always in the middle. The lion was more likely to select his meal from somewhere on the edge!

Then to even more shame I began to think, if I'm among the good soils, who are all these other people? An example of the hard path was almost certainly one of my aunts. She made no secret of her view that *'all this religion is a load of rubbish'*. If the seed of the Gospel was ever cast in her direction it would bounce like water off the proverbial duck's back. And I could easily think of a few shallow people I knew. They'd get all enthusiastic about something and would talk about nothing else. But although they started so much, they never finished anything before getting bored and moving on to the next craze. Then there were the weedy people. Not weak and spindly, but those whose lives were cluttered by 'things'. At home we had more than our fair share of 'things', including a TV with doors and a radiogram. But these were all essentials to life, were they not? A line had to be drawn and this our family did with a common mind. Electric carving knives and dishwashers were deemed beyond the pale. Anyone who aspired to owning such unnecessary luxuries would undoubtedly be quite incapable of producing anything of value in their lives. How could they, as they would far rather stay at home to look after their possessions than go to church? To my mind they probably wore shiny suits and sold second hand cars somewhere in South London.

When in my mid teens I really began to take God seriously, a number of things happened. Among them, the Bible came alive to me in a new way. I could hear Jesus speaking to me as never before. The trouble is, some of what he was saying shook what I'd thought was all sorted, including this parable. The problem came as I heard afresh those other challenging words of Jesus;

*"Judge not that ye be not judged." Matt.7:1* Who was I to dare judge these people in this way? And as I grew older I began to appreciate how bad parenting, tragedy, illness and many other negative life experiences outside our control can have such a bearing on who we become.

For example there was Margaret, a lovely lady in the church choir but well known for starting things and not seeing them through. Yet she was great with us young people, such fun, until that is she had what was called a 'nervous breakdown'. Was I really to consign her in my mind to being 'shallow soil' with no hope of a harvest? I began to seriously doubt my judgement and just how much good soil there was in my life. And yes, I found myself thinking I just don't believe this parable can possibly mean what I always thought it did. Yet what else could Jesus be saying?

This is one of those rare occasions in the Bible when a parable is explained. Mostly they are simply delivered and we are meant to work out what it means for us. It's rather like someone being asked to explain a joke, never a good idea and akin to pulling the legs off a frog, only to find it doesn't jump so well! In my more radical moments I have seriously wondered whether Matthew was right in including this explanation. In the text, we read it was after Jesus had gone back inside with his disciples that they asked him to explain it to them. If the conversation took place behind closed doors, how wise is it to include it in a book that anyone might read? Having said that, I realise if we were take that line with all the Bible we would lose many wonderful chapters, not least those in John where Jesus is alone with his disciples. At the very least, I believe it should cause us to read this explanation with care, for unfortunately it could easily seem to be saying that all these different sowing situations equate to different categories of people. What only adds to our dilemma is the modern obsession with putting one another into boxes. In many cases these days, if you won't go into a box, you can't join the system.

I can't say exactly when some light began to dawn, but during training I do remember studying parables and how they were meant to work. The first rule was to get the title right. The sub headings we read in modern Bibles are not part of Scripture but what the editors think the parable is primarily about. The title that Jesus intended is there in the opening words, as with a fairy story; *"Once upon a time there was..."* In a parable it often takes the form; ***"The Kingdom of heaven is like..."*** In the case of The Sower, we have actually got this one right, for it begins with the words; ***"A sower went forth to sow..."*** In other words, it is primarily about the sower. The problem comes when we think it's primarily about 'us and them'.

But this is no ordinary sower, the kind that everyone listening to Jesus would have been familiar with. We gardeners may think seed prices today are outrageous but seed has always been precious, not least in Jesus' day. And they would assume any farmer would know his land down to the last square inch. So to happily throw good seed onto bits you knew were hard paths, soil with rock just below the surface or full of weed roots was surely reckless. Yet this is the image Jesus suggests equates to 'Farmer God'. He is quite prepared to throw out countless opportunities for us to receive his grace and bear fruit, even when he knows his efforts will so often be wasted.

This picture of a recklessly generous God helped me to the second key that threw a whole new light on this parable. Taking to heart Jesus' command, *"Judge not..."*, I began to think, what if this parable is less about different types of people and more about the different degrees of success with which any of us may respond to the many opportunities God gives us? Apart from it being so invidious, and frankly untrue, to assume all the failed situations apply to someone else, there's nothing worse than a Christian who gives the impression they've got it all together. There's a real danger here for those in leadership. When I was installed as Chaplain at Carisbrooke Priory, a wise nun said to me; *'Don't let them put you on a pedestal.'* to which I felt bound to add; *'And don't let me encourage them to give me a leg up.'* Sadly it can be a mutual conspiracy. Leaders may mistakenly feel they must never admit to, still less show their weaknesses. They may even come to believe their own publicity! And some of us love to be able to tell everybody, we have the best pastor in town. But others in the congregation who seek to live with rather more honesty, look at these apparent paragons of holiness and may be tempted to feel thoroughly discouraged and hopeless. For them, so much of their own life of faith is by comparison lived in a fog. So I suggest again what value there may be in seeing the main thrust of this parable as being God's amazing generosity and how we each respond to it, even emulate it.

I admit it is just possible some people may be all hard path, nothing but shallow soil or totally infested with weeds. But the fact remains, none of us are in a position to judge one another in such a way. The Lord alone knows each of our hearts to its core and he will judge as only he can, according to his love, mercy and wisdom. Rather than us peering judgmentally over our neighbour's fence and criticising his gardening efforts, I suggest this parable is actually saying; *'Never mind about him for now. Get on and deal with the bit I've given you to look after'.*

Let's look at these 'sowing situations' in reverse order. I don't know about you, but if I'm honest my faith levels tend to fluctuate pretty wildly, depending on a whole load of factors. In my better moments I may have been inspired by another Christian, refreshed by a brilliant retreat or for some other reason find myself on a mountain top. My faith is elevated and I find myself more able to recognise and receive the seed the Lord sows my way. Encouraged by others, I may see it germinate, grow and produce a harvest many times greater than the seed sown. But on the other hand circumstances can change on coming down from the mountain top. Then I may find the cares of my world growing rather more vigorously than the crop, so as to choke out the good intentions. Similarly I might get 'spiritual cold feet', beginning to wonder if God has really given me enough faith to move the mountain after all. And having insufficient root, that particular seed of an opportunity withers and dies. And I'm not only thinking here of grand plans or long term visions. Some of the seed is, I believe, designed to grow and fruit in the twinkling of an eye.

Imagine the scene. Jack is a regular sort of Christian and he's late for the home group that he's due to lead this evening. It's been a long time waiting for his turn to come and he's put a lot into the preparation. He reckons he's been inspired and has some great ideas that will really impress everyone. He can't wait. The doorbell rings. It's his neighbours. They have a crisis and need help. It won't actually take that long to invite them in for a few minutes and listen to them. And even if Jack himself can't do anything for them he could maybe call up someone who can. But he's so keen not to be late and run the risk of someone else taking his place, he's rather short with his neighbour and leaves them standing on the doorstep, no nearer solving their crisis and feeling even worse for having bothered such an important person.

It takes longer to set this imaginary scene, than it would to actually play it out. One can imagine the divine hand of the Sower dropping the seed of an opportunity across Jack's path, the chance to show a bit of Christ-like grace. But on this occasion his heart is hardened by self interest, so down swoops the enemy and snatches the seed away. God willing there will be many other such opportunities, but this particular one is lost forever. It may not be until eternity when Jack fully realises just what a harvest of blessing could have come to his neighbours and himself, if only his own heart had been more receptive to the seed that God had sought to sow in it. The last thing though I believe the Lord would want, is for us to endlessly chastise ourselves over all the opportunities that we messed up through self interest, fear or simply being inattentive. But that's not to say, when he draws these things to our notice the right response should not be a prayer of confession and if appropriate, an apology, which will bring peace to all concerned.

I suggested the explanation of this parable in Matthew could seem to bear out the regrettable interpretation, that it is simply about different types of people and that we must decide where we and others fit in. As I have thought more carefully about this, my conclusion is this need not be so. When Jesus says *"These are those who do this."* and *"These are those who do that"* I am now much happier to read it as; *"This is what happens when you do this"* and *"This is what happens when you do that."* Yet when all is said and done, there must be a place for taking a wise and caring interest in someone else's walk of faith. Such is the role of a pastor, counsellor, spiritual director or simply a good friend. But I would suggest to fulfil well any of those privileged roles, we need first to consider with humility these other words of Jesus;

*"Why do you look at the speck of sawdust in your brother's eye and pay no attention to the plank in your own eye? How can you say to your brother, 'Let me take the speck of sawdust out of your eye', when all the time there is a plank in your own eye? You hypocrite, first take the plank out of your own eye, and then you will see more clearly to remove the speck from your brother's eye." Matt 7:3-5*

When it comes to the Parable of the Sower, the message to Victor Meldrew, or any of us for that matter must be *'If the cap fits, wear it!'*

## POSTSCRIPT

One of the other principles for understanding parables is that they are only intended to teach one thing. Any interpretation should elucidate that single point. At risk of contradicting myself, I am tempted to look at this parable both as a gardener and as one who has been involved in Christian healing for several years. Why is the path hard, where did the weeds come from and can we do anything about shallow soil? Paths are hardened by other people walking all over the soil and as such you can hardly blame the soil for that. Similarly weeds have a habit of just turning up. But if one is not careful you could begin to think the farmer himself has something to answer for. Is it not his job to deal with the weeds and at least avoid sowing where he knows the soil to be hard or shallow? Hence the need to keep focussed on the main point of the parable, which is the extraordinary generosity of the farmer that should in turn cause us to rejoice and be filled with hope. But we can of course allow the farmer to break up the hardened soil, assuming there is another route for the path to take. We can work with him in rooting out the weeds and it is possible for underlying rocks to be removed or at least to deepen the depth of the topsoil over them. All of which I believe adds a legitimate dimension to this teaching of Jesus. Yes, God is amazingly patient and faithful in sending countless opportunities for growth our way. But he is also the gardener in whose skilful hands, even the most unpromising areas of our life can be cultivated, so as to bring about a harvest we may have never dreamt of.

QUESTIONS

1. How have you always interpreted this parable?

2. Do you recognise Jack?

3. What else might have hardened the path?

4. Are you aware of any weeds you'd particularly like to get rid of?

5. How do you imagine God might increase the depth of topsoil?

6. What do you think the harvest is?

POEM

The fast train from Sevenoaks to London could be seen as an object lesson in 'judgmentally peering over your neighbour's fence'. You start from home surrounded by beautiful farmland before plunging into a tunnel that opens out into the other world of South London. Gradually the houses beside the track become smaller and scruffier, whilst the temptation increases to look down on the occupants. I'm not saying everyone who commutes from Sevenoaks thinks like this, but I have a kind of feeling it's a cap that may occasionally fit. I wrote this in the eighties when living in Sevenoaks.

## FIRST CLASS

From the orbit of the city
where the country meets the town,
where the morning air is sweetened
by the scent of garden flowers;
smartly suited gentlemen
with neatly folded papers,
join the train that leaves
just past the hour.

Parallel lines
head in the Times
pull down the blind
shut off the mind.

As the peaceful fields diminish
and suburban roads encroach,
like suffocating tentacles
that close around the throat;
passive rows of passengers
look blank with tunnel vision,
whilst the silence of unknowing,
settles thick upon the coach.

Parallel lines
head in the Times
pull down the blind
shut off the mind.

Speeding on towards the centre
where the wheel of fortune spins,
'Thank God it isn't stopping
so that they'll be getting in';
avert your eyes from looking
as the slipstream bares the backs
of the squalid little terraces
beside the lofty track.

Parallel lines
head in the Times
pull down the blind
Terminus.

# CHAPTER THREE

# HARRUMPH !

*"A man with leprosy came to him and begged him on his knees, 'If you are willing, you can make me clean.' Filled with compassion, Jesus reached out his hand and touched the man, 'I am willing. Be clean!' Immediately the leprosy left him and he was cured. Jesus sent him away with a strong warning: 'See that you don't tell this to anyone. But go, show yourself to the priest and offer the sacrifices that Moses commanded for your cleansing as a testimony to them.' " (Mark 1:40-44)*

Margaret Tarrant was a popular artist in the early part of the last century and her pictures of Jesus have hung on many a wall, including I confess our own. They have a certain sweet charm about them; Jesus in his white flowing robes surrounded by smiling children and baby animals. But apart from his very un-Jewish blond hair and blue eyes, I had a growing feeling this was an image in which I found it increasingly difficult to believe. There's no denying his tenderness, especially with some of the more vulnerable people he met. But there was another side to Jesus, most obviously when he upended the tables in the Temple and drove out the stall holders. I cannot miss the opportunity to say, this was not because Jesus objected to 'selling things in church', though as a Parish Priest I've had just such a view brought to me by those bothered about the Church Bookstall. Our Lord's problem was with those who used a privileged position to rip off their customers and worst of all to do it in his Father's name. I remember well Robert Powell's vivid acting of this scene in Zefirelli's film 'Jesus of Nazareth', his face contorted with anger and wielding a big stick. And yet there's something in us that is very uncomfortable with such a raw portrayal of Jesus.

This discomfort is nothing new. Some of the Gospel writers themselves seem to want to play down the angry, frustrated Jesus. We can deduce this best from Mark, who is generally thought to be the earliest writer and probably still a young man at the time. Some of the best examples are to be found in the passage that heads up this chapter. Mark seems to be writing in a hurry and this together with his un-cautious youthfulness causes him to tell it as it is and give us rather more of the passionate, human side of Jesus than Matthew, Luke and John. Even the translators seem to have got cold feet at times. It's not just over the Cleansing of the Temple but if we study the text carefully there are repeated instances in this and other accounts of Jesus' healing ministry, where most translations tend to avoid portraying too 'earthy' a Jesus. I have to come clean here and admit to being no Greek scholar, nor much of any kind of a scholar come to that. My reading list has always been pretty slim. But there is one book on Christian healing that for me stands head and shoulders over anything else I've read on the subject: "Jesus' Healing Works and Ours" by Ian Cowie.

As a Church of Scotland minister he looked after three industrial parishes before becoming Chaplain to the Christian Fellowship of Healing in Edinburgh for twelve years. I love his blend of fresh Biblical insight, observation from life and if necessary an honest admission of 'not knowing'. All this is in the context of an obvious love for and belief in his Lord Jesus. He retranslates the original Greek, often bringing out nuances overlooked in the versions we're familiar with. He seems to be especially fond of Mark's direct and gritty portrayal of the Son of God. Before we look at the man healed of leprosy, let us first consider the healing of the deaf and mute man who they brought to Jesus after he returned to Galilee;

*"There some people brought to him a man who was deaf and could hardly talk and they begged him to place his hand on the man. After he took him aside, away from the crowd, Jesus put his fingers into the man's ears. Then he spat and touched the man's tongue. He looked up to heaven and with a deep sigh said to him, 'Ephaphtha!' (which means 'Be opened!') At this the man's ears were opened, his tongue was loosened and he began to speak plainly."* (Mark 7:31-37)

I've always been intrigued by this passage, especially the bit about Jesus spitting, and wondered what place there might be for this practice in present day Christian healing. There's one for Health and Safety! I've also treasured one of those few occasions when we get the actual Aramaic word that Jesus used and this one is so full of expression. But first let's consider who brought the man, probably his family or friends. Given his condition, the man himself would have been unlikely to have the confidence or ability to approach Jesus on his own.

But straightaway we discover here is no gentle Jesus, speaking soft and consoling words to them. Most versions, including the NIV quoted above tell us that Jesus *"took him aside from the crowd"* but the actual word is something far stronger and more accurately translated as; *"grabbed him vigorously"*. It's the same word used to describe how the Lord grabs hold of Peter trying to walk on the Sea of Galilee before he goes under. This is no Sergeant Wilson from *'Dad's Army'* asking politely; *"Would you mind coming this way please? Would the rest of you mind waiting over there?"*

We also read how they didn't just ask Jesus but instead *"begged him"* to place his hand on the man inferring that Jesus was for some reason being hesitant. What could possibly lie behind Jesus' apparent reluctance to help and this odd way in which he grabs the man and unceremoniously drags him away from his loved ones? We can only speculate, but from observing life, where someone in a family is severely disabled, it's so easy for them to become over dependent and for the family to become over protective. It could be, in this instance, Jesus knew he had to do something bold and assertive to break these bonds that had become unhealthily restricting. One can imagine the Lord being eager to treat the man as an individual and encourage him to engage personally with him, rather than simply remain a passive recipient or, worse still, have all the questions he's asked answered for him by others. Jesus knows well this man needs not only to be healed from his obvious physical handicap. He needs also to receive a deeper healing that will involve discovering how precious he is to God and the purpose God has for his life, two things he's probably long since lost sight of.

Another curious word Mark uses here is *"grunt"* but most versions have it as Jesus *"sighing deeply"*. To my mind, that reinforces all the worst images of a rather effete figure, holding up one hand and resting the back of it on his forehead in a melodramatic gesture. *"Grunt"* on the other hand is far more earthy and so unusual, one can't help feeling Mark is recalling exactly what he saw and heard. As any one who has had anything to do with Christian Healing knows, it can often be very hard work. If we are to truly see it as engaging with Jesus' active, loving concern for the one in distress, it may well be emotionally, physically and spiritually draining. This 'grunt' from Jesus suggests huge exertion on his part as he removes whatever it is that has been keeping this poor man bound.

But there's another word Mark alone uses here and on a number of other occasions in his Gospel, for which there is no simple English equivalent. Elsewhere he uses it to describe the disciples' objection to the woman pouring the expensive perfume on Jesus' feet. Most version say they *'grumbled'*, the word actually used is much stronger and implies anger. Mark uses the same word to describe Jesus' reaction to the death of his dear friend Lazarus. In Greek it is the word used to describe the snort of a war horse. As such *"harrumph!"* is probably as near as we can get. At this point I have to say it's rather easier to explain this when speaking rather than writing so I'm afraid you'll just have to imagine me doing my impersonation of a snorting war horse! It is resonant with frustration, anger and offence in the face of something that should not be as it is. As such, it is not a thousand miles from Victor Meldrew's signature outburst of; *'I don't believe it!'* As with the deaf and mute man, we read that Jesus is begged for healing by the leper, suggesting once again an unexpected reluctance on his part. Jesus' reply cannot be more abrupt, to the point and one might almost say curt; *"I am willing. Be clean!"*

Immediately before he says this, the NIV, along with most versions tells us he was *"filled with compassion"* which is doubtless true but once again not quite the whole story. The word used definitely carries with it the sense of indignation. In fact the New English Bible has it as *'in warm indignation'* which is rather quaint and very English! But at least it is not seeking to conceal the evident sense of Jesus' frustration and anger. Those who opted for the safe and respectable *"with compassion"* deny us, I believe, a truer picture of the very real humanity of Jesus. This idea of indignation suggests the Lord is picking up a disturbing element of faithlessness on the part of the man. This is borne out by what follows. The version I quote here has Jesus; *"sending him away with a strong warning."* Once again the translators' reluctance to expose the strength of emotion is evident. Jesus did not just *"send him away"*. The Greek literally means *"He threw him out"*! Similarly *"with a strong warning"* tends to understate what actually happened, for this is where Mark describes Jesus as *"snorting" (harrumph!)* So according to Ian Cowie the more faithful translation of Mark at this point is; *"Snorting (harrumph!), he immediately threw him out…"*

I apologise if all that seems a bit of a conundrum, but I do believe it important we go as far as we can to understand the exact words in which the Gospels are written. If it offends by challenging our cosy picture of Jesus so much the better. I can almost hear Jesus responding to our wounded sensibilities with a loud *'harrumph!'* Far from being offended, I find this both refreshing and exciting. It confirms what I have in my heart always felt to be true, that the Son of God really did become fully human. He shares our frustration in the face of injustice, unnecessary suffering and all that is wrong in life. All these things and more may stand in the way of people really entering into the life that God always meant them to have. Jesus quite rightly is offended at these and so should we be. He wants us to be free of them and he is the One above all others who can now make that possible.

POSTSCRIPT

There is just a brief but important PS this time. Having a love of words, I admit I've enjoyed speculating in this Chapter at just how down to earth Jesus really was. To be fair, others who are fluent in Greek may well have another point of view. That is after all one of the reasons why we have so many different versions of the Bible and I do believe God speaks to us through all of them. Although they may differ in the words they use, what is more important and common to all of them is that these stories tell of Jesus working wonderful miracles of healing in people's lives. By faith and from experience, let me finish by saying with confidence, he still does!

QUESTIONS

1. If someone asked you why Jesus threw out of the temple the money changers and sellers of doves, what would you say?

2. Is there anything you can think of about our church today that might cause Jesus to do the same?

3. Are you comfortable with the idea of Jesus being angry,

frustrated, grabbing people violently and being reluctant to help when asked?

4. What makes you go *'harrumph!'*? Do think Jesus would have the same reaction?

5. Should we copy Jesus and use spitting as part of Christian healing?

POEM

We have been looking at the importance of how we portray Jesus, not least through the words that are chosen. This is especially significant when a word in ancient Greek can require many words of contemporary English to bring out all the nuances. And it is similar with painting and sculpture. For many centuries it was not considered right to depict Jesus showing emotion. The first paintings to do that, around a thousand years ago, were thought scandalous at the time. Later in Renaissance Italy, the technique of perspective was discovered, bringing literally a whole new dimension to how we represented Jesus. And there is a sense in which all art is artifice. All things considered, I've often thought it something of a miracle that two thousand years on, we can still encounter the authentic Christ. My belief is we can through the ongoing inspiration of the Holy Spirit, not least if we call upon him when revisiting the original Gospels that write of him.

## VICTIM OF PERSPECTIVE

You made me look at you
through eyes of Prussian blue,
oxidising now with passing time.

You hung me here,
so you can take your point of view
and stare at me.

You call this reality,
two dimensions pretending they are three,
playing tricks with my geometry.

You call this Renaissance,
a dawning into light,
so was I then a child of darkest night?

You no longer see
as those who saw
and first portrayed me

painting with a pen
and not a brush
on flat papyrus.

# CHAPTER FOUR
# ORIGINAL SIN
## (AN INTERNAL DIALOGUE)

When Adam and Eve ate the forbidden fruit, how would you describe what happened to them? Did God curse them?

No, he doesn't curse them. He curses the serpent and he curses the ground but he doesn't curse either Adam or Eve.

Yet he seems to be pretty hard on them. He ejects them from the Garden of Eden, tells Eve she will suffer pain in childbirth, that Adam will now eat by the sweat of his brow and both of them will in due course die and end up as dust.

That's right. We've always been told that's the price of sin. We sin and God punishes us.

So if you're saying what God does to Adam and Eve is punishment, then what's the crime and more's the point does the punishment fit the crime? Bear in mind not only are they cast out of the Garden and left to fend for themselves but all their descendants for time immemorial including you and me are liable to suffer the same punishment. Rather stiff, one might say, for a bit of scrumping.

Now you're being facetious. It was far more than a 'bit of scrumping'. They were wilfully disobedient and did what God expressly told them not to do.

Are you telling me you never once wilfully disobeyed your parents? And anyway, what kind of a parent, at the first offence,

48

throws their child out of its home, tells them to look after themselves from now on and refuses to hear any plea for mercy? So much for 'three strikes and you're out'! I always believed the Lord I worshipped to be like the Psalmist said; *"Compassionate and gracious, slow to anger, abounding in love." (Psalm 103:8)*

But if you're saying what Adam and Eve did, didn't matter then why did Jesus have to leave heaven, come to earth and die in agony on a cross?

I'm not saying it didn't matter. I believe it mattered a great deal to God. Straightaway he went looking for Adam, even though as the all-seeing, all-knowing One I can't help thinking he must have known where he was all the time. It rather depends on how you read it:

(With a gruff, angry voice)
*"Adam, where are you? Come out of there! Don't think I can't see you!*
*I have a bone to pick with you my lad - or should I say... an apple core?"*
Or
(With a more tender, concerned voice)
*"Adam where are you? I'm so sad you feel you need to hide from me. We always used to be so close, no secrets. You must be feeling just as bad as I am. Don't forget, I did make you in my image."*

No, it mattered alright. What started out as a 'bit of scrumping' (yes, sorry, I thought that would get you going), so should I say, a broken relationship with God eventually led to one of their sons murdering his brother. Let's agree to forget about scrumping. This is serious, a matter of life and death, literally. I think at the heart of it all is a question of belief in God or rather a lack of it. Adam and Eve were tempted to believe what the serpent said rather than what God had said. For what God in effect said was:

*"If you eat of the Tree of the Knowledge of Good and Evil you will surely die"* The serpent said: *"No you won't"*. Eve chose to believe the serpent rather than God and tried some. Trouble is she didn't die. Not straightaway at least. Then she offered some to Adam saying *"Look, I'm not dead."* and so Adam believed Eve and he ate some and he didn't die either. But God was right all along. They both did die, they had to and I'll tell you in a moment why I think that was. First though, if what God did to them was punishment, then what he said to them must have been a threat: *"Eat that and you're going to die."* On the other hand if what God allowed to happen to them was simply consequence then *"Eat that and you will die"* is what any loving parent would say when sending their children out in the garden to play, where strawberries and deadly nightshade grow together. No, I believe it's far more to do with consequence than punishment.

What do you mean, the consequence of what?

The consequence of growing up and becoming adult. Whatever else this story is about, I suggest it could be seen as a vivid depiction of the experience we all go through when we grow up and lose our innocence. At the risk of your glasses steaming up, just think for a moment about those fruits hanging 'right in the middle of the Garden'. All summer long, Adam and Eve play nakedly and innocently in the Garden but come the autumn and the fruits begin to ripen and all of a sudden they look very attractive and rather tasty! The consequence of Adam and Eve discovering each other sexually, would have been that they had to die. Not as punishment, but as an inevitable consequence. All the time there was just the two of them, they could live there forever, the Garden would sustain them. But now it could only be a matter of time before the Garden, and eventually the whole world, would become overpopulated to the extent that no one could survive.

And with the loss of innocence comes responsibility. If a two year old lashes out and injures someone, it's a tragedy. If a twenty two year old does the same, it's a crime. With growing up comes the power to make life and destroy life. And God knows how true that is.


POSTSCRIPT

This is my attempt to tackle one of the bigger issues exercising Christians today, a revisiting of the traditional teaching about The Fall and Original Sin. Augustine was a major leader of the early church and his teachings are not only still around but also remain influential. He is largely responsible for developing the doctrine of Original Sin, in a way that has influenced Christians for seventeen hundred years.

The story of the Garden of Eden clearly tells of something going seriously wrong between man and God, but the interpretation has to remain open to discussion. There's reason to be concerned about the interpretation Augustine puts on it, especially considering 'where he was coming from'. He was converted when still a passionate young man, with an eye for the ladies, as he confessed in his own writings. Clearly his heart and mind were converted at baptism, but it is reasonable to imagine his hormones took a while to fall into line. Taking a vow of celibacy, one cannot help but wonder if all this did not influence his attitude to women. What ever the reason, I cannot help but think it regrettable how he lays the blame primarily on Eve as the 'temptress of man', and so helped shape the church's attitude to all women from that point on. He may well have been speaking out of the values of his time, but I do believe our attitude to women in the church is finally being restored and for that I thank God. Of great interest to me is the compelling evidence that for the first few centuries, women commonly held positions of leadership in the church, including that of bishop.

When it comes to Original Sin, I'm not going to pretend it's all done and dusted for me. But in an odd way, I found it useful to put the thoughts going round my head in the form of a dialogue. In this postscript I want to add a few more, which you may find helpful, especially if you are going to attempt the questions that follow.

A question many ask about Genesis 1-3 is *"Is it true?"* by which they mean, *"Did it really happen?"* To my mind this is something of a red herring. It has to be a position of faith since no amount of archaeology is going to prove it one way or the other. For some Christians, *"Is it true?"* means, *"Is it true to life?"*, thus avoiding endless, fruitless arguments since even Aesop's fables are true to life. Let's make a plea here to those Christians who hold opposing views on this, that we agree to differ and allow one another whatever interpretation we feel right with. In defence of , *"Is it true to life?"* I would say that 'Adam' means literally 'man' or if you like 'Everyman', so it could be argued this story is as much about all of us, as about our first ancestors.

I have to admit to a Scriptural problem in seeing this as an account of the creation of all mankind, for if so, where did the people come from who inhabited the cities of the plain to which Cain was banished? For that and other reasons, I warm to the idea of this being the account of God's creation of the Adamic race, through whom he will ultimately bring Jesus, the Saviour of all the world. The only problem comes if we interpret *"being made in God's image"* as therefore only applying to this chosen race. Such exclusivity has given theological justification to some of our more shameful past, such as slavery and the practice cynically referred to as 'ethnic cleansing'. But such a conclusion need not be drawn, indeed I suggest should not be drawn. I am happy to believe that God would have created all the first human beings in his image and that all future generations can at least potentially reflect that image. Regardless of Evolutionary theory, one can see that people of every race share certain noble qualities with all humanity, qualities that are not found in the rest of the animal kingdom and could therefore be regarded as aspects of the image of God.

QUESTIONS

1. What's your take on the story of Adam and Eve? (If you find things getting too hot, please try 'agreeing to differ' or else leave this question until last!)

2. Why do you think God did not curse Adam and Eve?

3. How do your hear; *'Eat that and you will die?'*

4. How do you hear; *'Adam where are you?'*

5. Why did Jesus die? (You may find similar problems as with question 1 - but stick with it. It's really important, believe me!)


POEM

Do you like snakes? I confess I find them fascinating, not forgetting that 'fascination' is the word used to describe how a cobra transfixes its prey, just before striking. Satan appears as the serpent in the Garden of Eden. From what I understand, Satan was a masterpiece of God's creation, the Angel of Light. Sadly, as I suggest in this poem, his beauty led to his downfall. Snakes are beautiful, but beware!

## POOR SNAKE?

Poor snake?
so sinuous,
so elegant and lithe;
for sin you are
condemned to eat
the dust in which you writhe.

Poor snake?
a masterpiece
created with such care;
yet cast aside
since foolish pride
had caused you to be hypnotised
as some still, dark primeval pool
returned your haughty stare.

Poor snake?
the legacy
of beauty still remains,
for though despised,
all those with eyes
may see behind your slippery lines,
your Maker's many pains.

Poor snake?
who thought that you
would supersede the Lord,
would so deceive
the mind of Eve,
now find the God you would relieve,
still has the final Word.

# CHAPTER FIVE
# SIN AND SUFFERING

*"As he went along, he saw a man born blind from birth. His disciples asked him, 'Rabbi, who sinned, this man or his parents, that he was born blind?'*
*'Neither this man nor his parents sinned,' said Jesus, 'but this happened so that the work of God might be displayed in his life. As long as it is day, we must do the work of him who sent me." (John 9:1-4)*

This one ranks high in my tricky bits and I suspect I shall be scratching where a lot of folk are itching. I've picked out this passage from the healing of *'The Man born blind'* but will be referring to at least two others *'The Man on the Mat let down through the Roof'* and *'The Man on the Mat at the Pool of Bethesda.'* There are around thirty or so healing stories in the Gospels. In how many of those do you think 'sin' is an issue? The answer is three, these three, just ten per cent. Does that surprise you?

From our mother's knee, a lesson is learnt by most of us that sin brings suffering. If we are naughty we are punished, if we are good we are rewarded. Small wonder then, when later in life some tragedy comes our way, the cry goes up; *"What have I done to deserve this?"* Perversely it is possible for us to have acquired such an inaccurately low view of ourselves, far from even thinking such a thing, we may be tempted to believe instead; *"I should expect nothing less"*. More about that later but it is certainly true to say when something bad happens to someone good, the cry of outrage is pretty universal and more often than not aimed in God's direction. To be fair what he has revealed through Scripture may seem at times to bear this out. In the Wilderness, when the Israelites rebelled and told God and Moses they could keep their Promised Land and that they were sick of manna, we read in Numbers 21:6 that God sent venomous snakes among them. And in the New Testament, Paul puts it plainly; *"Do not be deceived. God cannot be mocked. A man reaps what he sows." (Galatians 6:7)* So we must conclude there can be a link between sin and suffering. But just how common, how inevitable, is it? Judging by the way so many of us react to problems and given a certain style of preaching still heard today, one would think the link is always there. In other words, if someone is suffering it is because they have sinned. The job of the Church, some believe, is to make them realise it and insist on a full, hearty and true repentance, together with the promise they'll never do it again. Or else! In relation to healing, the message is simply stated as, or perceived as; *"You're sick because you sinned. If you repent you'll be healed. If you don't, you won't"*. The trouble is some people repent and don't get healed. Others don't repent and yet God heals them.

I remember some years ago Frank, a Parish Priest we knew, took a house for duty at Groombridge on the Sussex/Kent border. Across the road from the Vicarage was Burrswood, the Christian Hospital and Healing Centre. Frank had not had any previous contact with the Christian healing ministry but was more than prepared to give it a go. He was immediately amazed at what he saw happen, such as one day when praying with a lady sent there by her family. *"I don't believe any of this mumbo jumbo."* was her frank exchange with Frank! Nonetheless he prayed and she was miraculously healed. The added twist in this tale was she left Burrswood soon after, saying, *"I still don't believe any of this mumbo jumbo."* One can only hope in time she did come to recognise the wonderful God who had healed her but there's no doubt it's an object lesson in grace, undeserved mercy. This whole subject is immense, so let us focus on Jesus and what he says and does in these three Gospel healing stories, where sin is specifically referred to.

The man born blind occurs only in John (Chapter 9) but is dealt with in great detail, including the Pharisees' sceptical investigation of the miracle. You may like to take the opportunity to read the chapter for yourself. But for now, it's the opening words that are most relevant. His disciples ask him; *"Rabbi, who sinned, this man or his parents, that he was born blind?"* Apart from the ludicrous idea that an unborn baby can be guilty of sin, what is yet more sad is they assume it must be one or the other. In other words, it must be sin that caused his blindness, so who's to blame? The answer Jesus gives is crucial, as is the version in which we read it. I have chosen the NIV, one of those more widely used. *"Neither this man nor his parents sinned."* Great. That's clear enough, although there's not much evidence the disciples took it in, nor the countless generations of us that followed. But just listen to what he then says; *"but this happened so that the work of God might be displayed in his life."* Now I'm sorry but this is where I reach for Victor's cloth cap and explode with indignation; *"I don't believe it!"* Is it really true that God has chosen to blind this baby from birth, in order that we may marvel in years to come when he heals him? That's not the God I love and worship. For years I was uncomfortable with this answer from Jesus, though never dared express it. I went all through the training and no one explained it. It was not until I read what Ian Cowie said that it became clear.

First let me remind you of the cuddly panda who eats shoots and leaves, or his gangster brother who goes into a café and eats, shoots and leaves. What a lot of difference a little comma can make. The trouble is, the Greeks never got round to inventing punctuation so what John literally writes is this; *"Neither this man sinned nor the parents of him but in order that be revealed the works of the God in him we must to work the works of the one who sent me while the day it is."* I'll invite you to read that again and admit it takes a bit of digesting. But remember, there is no punctuation. Only quite recently have translators included punctuation where they thought it should go. So you will find the meaning many Bibles put on it, is quite clearly; *"He was born blind so that the works of God might be revealed in him".* The great Bible scholar Campbell Morgan showed how very different this passage reads if we put the punctuation somewhere else;

*"Neither this man nor his parents sinned.* (Full stop) *But in order that be revealed the works of the God in him,* (Comma) *we must to work the works of the one who sent me while the day it is."*

So what John is, in effect, saying Jesus said is this;

*"Never mind speculating about who sinned - that is not the issue. Time is short and if the Glory of God is to be seen in this situation, I must get on with the work I've been given to do."*

Thank you Lord, I can live with that.

## The Lad on the Mat let down through the Roof

*"When Jesus saw their faith he said to the paralytic, 'Son, your sins are forgiven." (Mark 2:5)*

I'm picking out the key verse for now but would encourage you to read the full text again, in either Mark, Matthew 9:1-8 or Luke 5:17-26. On the face of it you might think this is all about sin. Some might say; *"Doesn't Jesus say so? Isn't that why this man is paralysed - with guilt? I reckon it's psychosomatic if you ask me."* Actually it's almost certainly not a man but a lad, what we would call a teenager, though such curious creatures were not invented in Jesus' day! According to Ian Cowie in his book, *'Jesus Healing Works and Ours'*, Mark and Matthew both use the word for 'lad', only Luke calls him a 'man'. That is, when all three of them are not simply calling him *'a paralytic'.* Three cheers for some of today's PC principles. Please, please let's not define one another by our problem. *'A young lad who was paralysed'* will do fine. It honours him as an individual, one who has an identity, outside of and beyond his condition. And that's what Jesus is about to do for him. But before he does, can you begin to imagine what is going through that poor lad's mind? I joke about there being no teenagers then, but in every culture as you grow from child to adult, it's always challenging. Hormones are rampant, your body is changing shape daily, most of the time you're feeling thoroughly gauche, self conscious and all too often guilty. This is especially true if you have those kind of ultra religious parents who have brought you up to feel you could never do anything right. How very paralysing that can be. I wonder, could that be the case here? In any event, you will have picked up what everyone else believes; that suffering is caused by sin. So as you have lain on your mat, with precious little else to do, you'll have been turning over and over in your mind just how sinful you must have been for God to do this to you. Well, you're certainly being punished for it now. No running with your mates, though you do have friends. But what sort of friends are these? The house where the rabbi is teaching is so full, they take you up on the flat roof, rip a hole in it and let you down in full view of everyone, right in front of the rabbi. How embarrassing is that? If only you could run away. What on earth is he going to say?

*"How dare you interrupt me! Look at the mess. Someone will have to pay for this. Why couldn't you queue like everyone else? Well, OK you're here now, so we'd better get on with it.'* Turning to the crowd, Jesus says; *"Now here's a fine example of what I was just telling you about, how sin is punished with suffering. Look at this lad - totally paralysed. I shall now list off some of the wicked sins he has been committing - especially the ones he thought I, the All Seeing One couldn't see him doing!"*

No. Jesus is not in the business of humiliating people publicly, even if sadly, some of us Christians are. Just look at what our Lord says to him, what he calls him. Not *'Paralytic'* but *'Son'*. It's the only place in the Gospels where Jesus refers to anyone as *'Son'*. Incidentally there's only one place in the Gospels where he refers to anyone as *'Daughter'* and that's *'The Woman with the Issue of Blood'*, who reaches out to touch the hem of Jesus' garment 77(Luke 8: 40-48). What this woman and the lad on the mat have in common, is how terrible they must be feeling about themselves. They believe they must be so sinful to suffer like this. And the woman knows well she is compounding the sin by mixing with the crowd in her unclean condition and worst of all, touching and so defiling a rabbi. In both cases Jesus addresses each of them with a word that instantly speaks to them of God's unconditional love. To him she is a daughter, to him he is a son. To the woman he says *"Daughter, your faith has healed you. Go in peace."* No mention of sin that she needs to confess. And to reassure the lad, Jesus declares that when it comes to sin, he really has nothing to worry about and so says to him; *"Son, your sins are forgiven."*

## The Man on the Mat at the Pool of Bethesda

Again I would encourage you to read the story for yourself in John 5:1-14. For now, I'll just highlight the closing words; *"Later Jesus found him at the Temple and said to him, 'See, you are well again. Stop sinning or something worse may happen to you." (Verse 14)* This is one of just two healing stories that involve a follow up, the other being the raising of Lazarus, when Jesus goes back for a party. *'Stop sinning'* is better translated, *'Don't go on sinning'.* So exactly what has he been doing that means Jesus has to warn him like this? Wouldn't we like to know! We can speculate, as we often do in such matters. The Pool at Bethesda is a pagan site. The man, we assume, was a fellow Jew, since Jesus found him again in the Temple. God's Law would forbid him from seeking healing through pagan beliefs or pagan rituals. So perhaps Jesus is saying to him; *"Don't dabble in things spiritual that you should not, or else you may end up in a worse state than before."* The truth is we don't know and all we can say is that, in this instance, Jesus knows the man has to do *something.* And we can be fairly sure the man would have known precisely what Jesus had in mind. Otherwise, you can imagine him living in terror, thinking that one naughty thought or letting slip a rude word, would find the wrath of God dropping on him from a great height. And what is even more important is that all this takes place after he his healed, not before and certainly not as a precondition of his healing. Out of love and concern for him, Jesus shows him where he is going wrong and encourages him to put things right with God, so as to be not only well but also truly healed and to stay that way too.

So where does all this leave us regarding the link between sin and suffering? I would suggest a far cry from where many of us too often are, especially when things go seriously wrong in our lives. I do think as a Church we need to look very carefully at our preoccupation with sin and repentance, not least when presented as a prerequisite of healing. How many times did Jesus say: *"You must first confess your sin and repent before I can heal you"?* or *"Your suffering is due to your sin".* Answer, none. Of course I believe there is a place for repentance, especially when understood as *'re-thinking'* which is what *'repentance'* literally means. The renewing of the mind, how we think about ourselves, others and God is at the root of much healing. But it can take time, even with God. At Carisbrooke Priory, where I was Chaplain for a number of years, we held a lot of store by a prophetic word brought in 1996, the second line of which reads: *'I am showing you my way of love - love that accepts, values, affirms and heals as the outcast is brought in.'* Accepts, values, affirms, heals. Where is the demand for owning sin, for admitting our need for forgiveness? From what I have seen over the years, most people who are outcasts are all too aware of their unworthiness and far more need to hear first that God will accept, value, affirm and heal them as they are. And God's love for them being what it is, he will not want them to remain as they are, but with him and in his own good time he will restore them to the person he always intended them to be.

But to return to this core issue; *'How much is our suffering due to our sin?'* and *'What did I/they do to deserve this?'* I look at the record of Jesus' ministry and can draw only one conclusion. He shows me that God does not want a relationship with us simply based on rewards and punishments, such as we might have with a member of the animal kingdom. He wants a relationship of love and belonging as between a father and son, mother and daughter, as children of the Kingdom of God. In his Kingdom, love transcends everything. It does not depend on circumstances. It is not a contract but a covenant. It is stronger than even death itself. We may not think we have it in us to love like that and to be honest we do not. Such love only comes from knowing Jesus, which is why, to live in such a relationship with God, he wants each of us to receive his love for ourselves.

QUESTIONS

1. How do we receive God's love?

2. What suffering can you think of that could be the result of sin?

3. What examples from Jesus' ministry can you think of that involve him healing someone before they have made a confession of sin and been forgiven?

4. How do you think the lad on the mat and the woman with the issue of blood felt when Jesus called them respectively 'son' and 'daughter'?

5. Why do you think so many people still believe suffering is mostly, if not always, caused by sin?

POEM

This one is a bit different. I've chosen *Dresden China* partly because I confess to being rather pleased with it, being the only one that ever got an award in a poetry competition. In tackling war, this is an especially complex issue when it comes to sin and suffering. I have much respect for those who hold to a pacifist view but at the same time, am truly thankful for the many who have suffered and died that we may enjoy the liberty we do. Ever since first learning about the bombing of Dresden, I, like many, have agonised over this tragic and controversial part of our history.

I use a little poetic licence. My mum actually worked in insurance, not a munitions factory and although dad was an officer in the RAF, it was of the dental kind. If you were a pilot in a dogfight you certainly didn't need the distraction of toothache, made even worse at altitude. And life was still full of danger for both of them, as they were living near Biggin Hill for part of the war. If it comes to that, I was not born until 1948. But the trauma of it all still somehow seems very close to home.

## DRESDEN CHINA

My eyes could barely see above
the scrubbed and polished table,
where my busy aproned mother
softly whistled as she ladled
the hot red flowing jam
to fill the crystal brittle jars.

My eyes could barely see beyond
the walnut Vauxhall dash,
nor the pride that drove me on
beside the figure of my dad,
as we headed for the Sussex coast,
just a single Summer past.

My eyes were never meant to see
the sequel to those days,
when a mother filled incendiaries
while the factory radio played,
and a father flew a Lancaster
toward a sleeping German town.

Through darkened leaded diamonds
from a darkened polished sill,
two neatly painted eyes
looked out
to see the falling fires of hell.

From the instant of the firing
on a distant, hectic day,
his glazed and modelled pose
stood still,
this tiny china boy.

Lead ran down in rivers
as the furnace roared again,
his limbs were split like peaches,
his complexion peeled away.

In the heat of retribution,
from the striking of a match,
the work of love is rendered down
to nothing more than ash.

# CLIFF HANGER AT NAZARETH

## LUKE 4: 14-30

By all means read the text, but for now please allow me to paint the picture. After his testing time in the Wilderness, Jesus has returned to the region of Galilee to start his ministry in earnest. People are amazed at his teaching and word spreads rapidly. He returns to his hometown of Nazareth and on the Sabbath goes to the synagogue. Probably because of what people are saying about him, he's given the honour of reading the Scriptures. Everyone would have been there, his mother, brothers and sisters, aunts and uncles, to say nothing of all those he'd grown up with and the older generations who remember him as 'Joseph's lad'. The pleasure and pride they must have all felt would have been heightened by the fact that this was Nazareth and this was 'our boy'. You see, there was a saying in those days that did the rounds. Nathanael, when it was first suggested he become a disciple of Jesus of Nazareth instantly trotted it out; *"Nazareth! Can anything good come from there?" (John 1: 46)* It's not easy living somewhere that everyone else thinks is rubbish. But it's just like God to have Jesus growing up there of all places. He seems to have a way of picking out the one that everyone else overlooks.

However there is another intriguing angle to this, presented by Richard A Batey in his book, *'Jesus and the Forgotten City.'* Just four miles north of Nazareth lie the ruins of Sepphoris. Recent excavations reveal a large, sophisticated cosmopolitan town, with colonnades, forum, theatre, villas and the palace of Herod Antipas. Although a Jewish town in a Jewish area, people from many other Mediterranean nations would have lived there, including Romans, Greeks and Phoenicians. The contemporary historian Josephus called it 'the ornament of all Galilee' and tradition has it as the childhood home of Mary. Also interesting is that it was destroyed by the Romans in 3BC, following a rebellion. Herod Antipas then set about rebuilding it, in a project that would have spanned all the early years of Jesus' life. It has long been appreciated that Jesus and Joseph were not so much carpenters as carpenter builders and it is impossible not to imagine they would have been closely involved in its reconstruction, apart from frequent trips to Sepphoris to visit granny and grandpa! All this gives the lie to the common impression that Jesus grew up knowing nothing but a remote, rural community.

And now years later and back in Nazareth, he's given the book of Isaiah to read. How many times I've found the set readings for the day to be amazingly relevant to something at the time. It's uncertain whether Jesus chooses the passage or it was chosen for him. All I do know, it would have been a different story if they'd given him Leviticus!

*"The Spirit of the Lord is upon me,*
*because he has anointed me to preach good news to the poor,*
*He has sent me to proclaim freedom for the prisoners*
*and recovery of sight for the blind,*
*to release the oppressed,*
*to proclaim the year of the Lord's favour."*
*(Isaiah 61:1-2a)*

Wow! You could hear a pin drop. And then, double wow, Jesus declares; *"Today this Scripture is fulfilled in your hearing".*

This Scripture had been around for well over six hundred years. Everybody knew how special it was and that it was all about the Messiah, the anointed Saviour that God would send. Now you would have thought that someone in the congregation might have a problem with this, maybe one of his relatives or that lad who used to live next door. They do say; *"Isn't this Joseph's son?"* but there's no sense of outrage or disbelief. Quite the opposite for they are amazed at the wonderful way in which Jesus spoke. They must have all thought *'YES! At last! Up to now it seems God only does special things down south, in Judah, around Jerusalem.'* It must have been like Cleethorpes being asked to host the Olympics!

Then something very strange happens. Jesus goes on speaking and suddenly they explode with rage. They drive him out of the synagogue and out of town, to the edge of a high cliff. Don't forget, Nazareth is a hilltop town overlooking a plain. They are determined to throw Jesus off the cliff, which is bad enough, but just remember who 'they' are. These are people he'd grown up with, worked with. I can't imagine any of his family members were baying for his blood, but it's odd that Luke doesn't even mention them trying to stop the crowd. Perhaps they were just overwhelmed, taken by surprise, as I think we all are. I've included this story, because I had always found it difficult to believe why his own people should turn on him so suddenly and so violently. If they really did believe he was the Messiah, why on earth try to destroy him? Here I must confess to having what I think may be an original thought. I don't remember having read it anywhere and certainly can't refer you to theologians who draw the same conclusion. Probably someone has, and it's down to my limited reading list. My ideas though have been much influenced by Russ Parker's book, 'Healing Wounded History' in which he explores how communities inherit shared memories. These memories can be a powerful agent for both good and evil. I'll let you read about one remarkable example of this in Russ's own words:

A certain incumbent was appointed to a group of ten churches in East Anglia. He set about his new ministry and in particular encouraged all ten churches to find ways of coming together for special occasions in order to build community and service to the needs of others. After a couple of years he noticed that one church in particular refused to take part in any of these social events. Eventually the Minister approached the Wardens of the church and asked them why this was so. He was told that it was because of the Vikings! The Minister could hardly believe this explanation as the event was 900 years earlier and surely had no currency in his day? The Wardens went on to explain that long ago when another Viking raid took place, because the people in the adjoining village had erected a high tower to look out for such eventualities, they were able to warn their own people but they did not warn the people in the neighbouring village. As a consequence the people in that village had not forgotten nor forgiven this event. As such it had fostered an ongoing attitude of mistrust to the neighbouring villages which had come down through the generations. Eventually the Minister felt that the only way to heal this breech of relationship was to go to that one village with the Wardens from the other churches and apologize for not warning them of danger so long ago. It was this act of repentance which became the foundation for that village changing its attitude to its neighbours and moving on together.

One of the extraordinary things about this story is that not all those present could possibly have been descendants. One can imagine parents instilling into their children certain beliefs and prejudices, but it seems complete strangers moving into the area were able to tap into and own for themselves the spirit of this ancient memory. In the Nazareth of Jesus' day were probably many families, whose roots had been there for generations and Jesus himself was a son of Nazareth. I suspect that as he grew up, he began to hear the community's story and parts of it dismayed him. Nazareth's problem, it seemed, was not with a neighbouring village, nor even another race of people, but with God himself. The two stories that Jesus reminded his people of, the ones that ignited their fury, concerned God doing miracles for foreigners rather than his own chosen people. In Elijah's day, the son of the woman from Zarephath in Sidon he raised from the dead, yet Israel was full of grieving widows at the time and he didn't do the same for any of them. In the case of Naaman, it was even worse. This man was the commander of the army that had just defeated them. Naaman contracted leprosy. *'Good'*, they must have thought at the time, *'that will be God's punishment. Serves him right!'* But no, even though Israel was full of lepers, God chose to heal Naaman!

I believe Jesus knew that his community had let these thoughts get imbedded in their collective heart and passed them on from one generation to the next. These were beliefs that basically said; *'God is not to be trusted, he's unjust'*. Jesus knew perfectly well how utterly wrong they were. He also knew, so long as these thoughts remained lodged in their hearts, they would never be able to receive the healing that, as their Saviour, he had been sent by God to bring them. For he knew they were impoverished, blinded, imprisoned and oppressed not least because of their lack of trust in God. It was like a vicious splinter deep in the flesh that had festered. The only way was to first give it a gentle squeeze but the pain was just too much and they lashed out. If Jesus had had a manager at that point, he would doubtless have been sitting there with his head in his hands saying; *'Oh Jesus, my boy, why did you have to go and say that? You had them eating out of your hands.'* But Jesus knew the only way was the way of truth and it was simply not true that God was not to be trusted. If those people of Nazareth, for whom he must have had a special love, were to receive the healing he had been sent to give them, they had to let the physician diagnose the cause of their sickness and be willing to receive the treatment he offerred.

I feel something has to be said about the darker, spiritual nature of all this, so far as we can comment with any certainty on things which are by nature hidden, that is occult. What is especially disturbing about this story is the violent rage these people suddenly expressed. It was as if they were taken over, possessed.

Perhaps they were. They wouldn't have been the only ones who heard Jesus declare the inauguration of God's Kingdom of healing and peace. The Enemy must have been fully aware what was happening and would have wanted to do his damnedest to nip this Messiah in the bud. And the kind of places the Enemy likes to inhabit are the deep, dark recesses of the human heart, where bitterness and disbelief in God are stored and nursed.

What Jesus brings to light at Nazareth is sadly true the world over. It lies at the heart of recurring violence and hatred between all kinds of warring factions. We look at places like Kosovo and Northern Ireland and indeed the Middle East itself and when things are at their worst may well cry out; *"Will it never end?"* The sad truth is it will not, so long as grievances are stubbornly held onto and passed on to the next generation. But the whole point of the Saviour coming is to say; *"I bring you Good News. It need not go on. I can change it. I can change you."* The message from Isaiah that Jesus brings is often read as applying to the individual, which of course it can. But it is every bit as relevant to families, towns, nations, races and creeds. The love of God in Jesus compelled him to bring this Good News first to the house of Israel, which he knew was so much in need of healing. Here in Nazareth, at the outset of his ministry, he was to see what a price he'd have to pay for offering the hand of healing to his own people. But his time to die was not then, so he was able to miraculously walk away from them. That time would come, and in the ultimate of paradoxes his death would mean life for all of us.


POEM

One of the fascinating things about the life of Jesus is how little we know about the majority of it, especially the early years. Apart from the Christmas story, which only two of the Gospels include, nearly all we know is summed up by Luke in these few words; *"And Jesus grew in wisdom and stature and in favour with God and men." (Luke 2:52)* I like William Barclay's view that what is so remarkable, is that it is so unremarkable. While waiting for the Father's call, Jesus basically got on with the job of being a good son and brother and probably the head of the family too when, as tradition believes, Joseph died while Jesus was still a young man. People have speculated as we are wont to do and as I have done in the following poem. I like to think though my offering is somewhat more Scriptural than the view of a work colleague many years ago who insisted the young Jesus travelled to India and studied at the feet of a guru. I think my friend was getting confused with John Lennon at the time!

CLIFFTOP AT NAZARETH


A cloudless day of heavenly blue
an early hour in early days
before the searing heat
had drawn the heavy haze
to mar the view,


A young boy stood
in solitude
to gaze.


At his waist the heads of grass
bowed with all creation,
stirred by the wind
that lifts his raven curls
and cools his face,
that lifts the watching eagle high
above the valley
far below.


Alone he'd lie
for hours on end,
a part and still apart;
looking up to scan the sky;
the floor of heaven,
sunlit rippled surface
of a pool seen from beneath.

And will he hear the whisper
in the wind and on the breeze,
Father's breath that carries word
from time to come?

"This is my Son,
the Son I love,
in whom I am
well pleased."

QUESTIONS

1. Are you aware of any ongoing problem in your family or your church that might be helped by applying the ideas behind 'Healing Wounded History'?

2. Were you always surprised by the reaction of the people at Nazareth to what Jesus said?

3. Look up the passage from Isaiah 61 that Jesus read. Why do you think he stopped where he did, half way through the sentence in verse 2?

4. Can you think of any circumstances in which any of us may be tempted to think, *"God is not to be trusted, he's not just"*?

# CHAPTER SEVEN
# THE LOST AND THE LOSERS
## LUKE 15

It could be useful to read Luke 15 first before we take, what I think you may find, is quite a different look at these three parables about being lost. I'm going to be asking two questions:
*What is absent from all three parables?*
*What is common to them, apart from the obvious?*

But before all that, we need to take note of the setting in which Jesus delivers this set of parables. We read how he is surrounded by tax collectors and 'sinners'. Now your view of the Inland Revenue may be that it is perfectly reasonable to lump them in with sinners. But to anyone who is employed by Her Majesty in this capacity, please be assured it is a thoroughly respectable profession and God loves you as much as any of us. But that's not what they thought in Jesus' day, for the taxes were those imposed by the occupying Roman government and any Jew who cooperated with 'the enemy' by collecting the taxes from fellow Jews was thought despicable. The Jewish teachers were sure God felt the same way, so sinners they were. In other cases, 'sinners' were only technically sinners, for example by reason of the job they did, especially if it was a bit mucky. This meant any decent, self respecting Jew would keep them at arms length and certainly never eat with them.

Shepherds were among those deemed 'sinners', which is ironic since Jesus was to call himself 'The Good Shepherd' and here he launches straight in with a parable about a lost sheep and a diligent shepherd. He is taking a well aimed swipe at those self righteous religious leaders who are sitting there tut–tutting at

Jesus, a rabbi who disgraced himself by eating with this unholy rabble. Some Bibles give each parable a title: *A lost Sheep, A lost Coin and a lost Son*. This is all very neat, but not in my view very accurate. As I said in Chapter Two, it is essential when reading a parable to understand who it is primarily about. Everything in the parable is designed to bring that out. And the title, what it is about, is to be found in the opening words which is then amplified in the text that follows. Applying that principle, these three parables are actually about;

*A **Shepherd** who lost a sheep- that he really cared for.*

*A **Woman** who lost a Coin- that was precious to her.*

*A **Father** who had two errant Sons - both of whom he loved equally and extravagantly.*

Not so snappy, but far more true I believe to the teaching Jesus always intended to convey. Commonly many of the parables are given titles that make us, rather than God the subject, which then easily leads to misinterpretation.

No points for suggesting 'loss' is common to all three but on the other hand what is quite different in each case is the culpability of what or who is lost. Depending on the degree of blame, we may be tempted to think *'Serves them right for getting lost'* as one might imagine the Pharisees did. Take the lost coin, which may have been out of the woman's housekeeping but more probably one of a bracelet of coins that had formed part of her wedding dowry. She was certainly keen to find it. But by no stretch of the imagination could you hold the coin responsible for losing itself. If anyone was to blame, it could have been whoever made the bracelet in the first place or the woman for being careless. It's not much different when it comes to sheep. A shepherd once told me that sheep all share two ambitions in life, that is to either escape or die! Fortunately, this shepherd that Jesus describes does not say *'Stupid thing, blowed if I'm putting myself out to find it'*. In the case of the two sons, it's not quite as simple as it may appear. It's certainly true the younger son is responsible for being lost, Jesus has the father saying as much. But what is clearly inferred from the story, and would have been very apparent to Jesus' audience at the time, is that his older brother is just as lost and probably more so. When the younger boy demands his share of the estate, he is in effect saying to his father; *'I wish you were dead.'* In due course, half of the estate would have come to him anyway and in that culture it was not unknown for a father to sign over his estate to his sons while still alive. The crucial thing is, it was the father's prerogative to do so. For the son to ask such a thing was the most insulting, disrespectful thing he could have said to his father.

What is not so apparent to us is how those listening to Jesus would have been just as shocked that his brother remained silent. As the older brother, it was his responsibility to defend his father's honour. Everyone would expect the older brother to remonstrate with his brother, but he says nothing. For that matter everyone would have expected the father to react with rage against his younger son and punish him severely for daring to ask such a thing. To everyone's amazement the father simply goes ahead and does it. Perhaps the old man is losing his marbles, in which case it would still be the older son's duty to protect the family's reputation and interests. But no, he keeps quiet and happily receives his half of the estate. His shame is compounded when his younger brother comes home, virtually from the dead. He rejects his father's invitation to come and join the party. Once again, as older son, custom demanded he was there to welcome the guests. By refusing to go, he was dishonouring the guests and his father. He falsely accuses his brother, who he pointedly refers to as *"your son"* of squandering the money on prostitutes. If true, his brother could have been stoned to death as punishment. But Jesus only said he'd spent it on *"wild living"*. And the whole tone of the older son is one of grudging self pity and lack of any love for his father, who he sees as mean for never letting him have as much as a young goat to share with his friends. This accusation is also false, for as the father says *"Everything I have is yours"*. In other words; *'Your brother had half and you had half. It wasn't me stopping you do whatever you wanted with your half*. But what matters most of all, is the tragic breakdown in relationship with his father as revealed by the older son, who is every bit as lost as his younger brother. In the story the younger boy is found, but we never know if the older son remained for ever lost to his father and his brother in his bitterness and resentment.

And so to the first of the two questions; *'What is absent from all three parables?'* I know that's almost an impossible question to answer, for it could be one of a million things. But that's why I add, *'that you might have expected to be there'.* I suggest what is glaringly not there is any sense of dwelling on the cost to the one who is doing the searching. Our shepherd as he trudges over hill and down dale might have been excused for muttering about how he could really do without this. Perhaps it came on to rain. Odds are the sheep has got itself either stuck in a thorn bush or half way down a cliff, in which case the shepherd could well be putting his own health or even his life at risk. And when he finds the sheep, does he complain about his poor back as he lifts the wretched, soggy animal on to his shoulders and carries it all the way home? The woman similarly seems remarkably restrained. There was probably no one around to listen, but it doesn't take much to imagine her grumbling; *'Isn't it just my luck? I've got a thousand and one things to do and now here I am, having to turn the place upside down. I don't believe it!'* But no, none of that. She simply gets on and searches carefully until she finds it.

In the third story, as any parent of a wayward child would know, it's the parent who suffers most. And can't you imagine him letting rip when the boy returns; *"Have you any idea what you've put your mother and I through? She never got over it, after you left like that. Of course you wouldn't know, she died last year, as if you cared. Your mother died of a broken heart. And you broke it."* That may all seem a bit melodramatic, but do you know I've heard the Gospel presented just like that. Going to the most extraordinary lengths, the preacher has set out to break people down. He was determined they should realise exactly how much they put God through, in coming to try and save them. Some years ago the BBC religious affairs correspondent, Gerald Priestland, recalled how, as a young boy, he was sent to boarding school. In the Chapel, the preacher would point at the figure of Jesus in agony on the cross and then spin round and stab his finger accusingly in the direction of the boys, with the words; *"You did that to Jesus."* Gerald admitted most of his fellow pupils simply let the words pass them by, but he was a sensitive lad and as time went on, the guilt became unbearable and caused him eventually to have a nervous breakdown. The resolution of this tragic story is that Gerald's healing was to come years later in Vienna, on the couch of a Jewish psychiatrist.

The father in the story Jesus tells could not be more different. With a touch of deep poignancy, it appears the father's eyes were forever trained on the horizon in the hope his missing son might one day return. In any event, when he does, the father's words and actions are an overwhelming display of unmitigated love and mercy. For a start the father runs out to meet him. Nothing special about that we might think, but not so to those at the time. Important people did not run in public and such action would be humiliating and seriously damage your reputation. What does this image remind you of? A man, a very important man allowing himself to be humiliated in full public gaze and with his arms outstretched? I would honestly say, if we had nothing but this parable, it would tell us all we need to know about who Jesus is and why he was crucified. The father goes on to cover his son with kisses. The Greek word means either, *"kissed effeminately"* or *"kissed again and again and again."* Which do you think it should be? Bearing in mind what it would mean to a Jew, the fact that the boy has been lately up to his neck in pigs, this image of self sacrificing love is absolutely staggering and I am lost for words.

And when it comes to the son, where is his repentance, his full realisation of the depth of his sin? Some say he repented before he turned for home. I disagree. Jesus says; *"He came to his senses"* which could mean no more than a rational response to feeling sorry for himself. He thinks to himself, *"My father has staff better off than I am. I'll go back and ask him to take me on as a hired man."* He realised he could never go back as a son, he'd blown that for good. Yet he didn't offer to become a slave, which could have indicated some remorse on his part. As a hired man he could come and go as he chose. The fact is though, as soon as his father sees him he runs to him, throws his arms around his son and smothers him in kisses. The boy doesn't get a chance to say a word of his carefully prepared speech. For all the father knew, his son had thought; *"My dad's a soft touch. I bet if I go back, he'll at least give me a job and somewhere to stay."* When he does finally speak, it is I believe through tear-filled eyes, utterly overwhelmed by his father's irrational, unconditional forgiveness and acceptance. The boy says; *"Father I have sinned against heaven and against you. I am no longer worthy to be called your son."* The father hears it and is no doubt glad to do so. But he says no more about it but instead declares eagerly; *"Quickly! We must have a party and celebrate."*

The last thing I want to suggest is that we should overlook the suffering of Jesus and our part as mankind in it. Of course not. But I do here express my appreciation of the traditional Church calendar. Each year we are directed at the appointed season to dwell on all the different aspects of this wonderful story from Creation to Revelation. Quite rightly in the days leading up to Easter, known in catholic circles as Holy Week our minds are focussed on the Passion of Christ. I remember at College first coming across 'The Reproaches' which are sung at this time. The simple, beautiful music adds immense power to those heart rending words from Lamentations; *"Is it nothing to you, all you who pass by?" (Lamentations 1:12a)* Every time I sing or hear them my heart is deeply moved. But they are only used during Holy Week, just one week out of fifty two. I really believe Jesus does not want us to continually reproach ourselves for what he went through on our behalf, though too many sermons I fear seem to have that as the default position. And I am also quite convinced such a challenging act of self examination is meant for those already securely rooted in him. It is certainly not for young impressionable children, nor I think for those who come tentatively seeking faith. In my experience those who have overcome so many obstacles to simply get over the threshold of a church often already have a deep sense of guilt and unworthiness. Far from 'rubbing it in', I believe our role as the Church is to emphasise what is so good about the God of the Good News. As someone once said, Jesus came not to rub it in, but rub it out.

All of which brings us to the second question. *What do these three parables have in common?* Apart from the word 'lost', there is one other word that runs through all three of them like a thread of pure gold and that is the word **'Joy'**. The diligent shepherd *joyfully* puts the sheep on his shoulders. He calls to his friends and neighbours; ***"Rejoice with me"***. Jesus goes on to say how much ***rejoicing*** there will be in heaven. The woman on finding her precious coin calls all her friends and neighbours together and tells them to; ***"Rejoice with me"***. And Jesus goes on to say how ***"There is rejoicing in the presence of the angels"***. One can imagine the woman throwing a huge party and spending many times what the coin was worth! And of course the joy of the father, who recklessly and irrationally loves both his sons, is overwhelming when the younger one returns. No recriminations, no demand for penance. Instead the father orders a great party. There is fatted calf, the best robe, and a ring on his finger; all things symbolising that the son is now a fully restored member of the family.

QUESTIONS

1. Look up some of the other parables. Does your version of the Bible give them titles? Do you think they are the right ones? e.g. as in Matthew 13, Luke 18

2. What have you always thought about the older son in *'The Parable of the Father who had Two Sons'*? Do you think he got a raw deal?

3. In the three parables of Luke 15, who are the losers?

4. How do you react when you lose something special to you?

5. What are some of the things that could cause us to get lost?


POEMS

There are two of them this time. The first is a slightly different take on 'The Lost Sheep', prompted by my experience of coming across a sheep half way down a Pembroke cliff, tangled up in bailer twine and brambles. After a few tentative efforts, I decided the prudent approach was to go and find the shepherd! The other is a reflection on what we often know as 'The Prodigal Son.' My understanding of this third and great parable was much influenced by a book I was introduced to at college. *'Poet and Peasant & Through Peasant's Eyes'* by Kenneth E Bailey which gives a wonderful insight to the parables of Luke.

## LATE ARRIVAL

As in a dream, it was, as if asleep
peacefully couched in sweet bedstraw,
ninety nine sheep
in the flock that I saw,
grazing safe on a warm summer's clifftop.

Deaf to the sound, they were, blind to the sight,
turned away were the soft woolly heads,
lost to the plight
unaware far below
of the sheep that was trapped on a ledge.

It would not go on and it could not go back,
stranded for so many years,
thrown as a lamb
it had grown up in fear,
ever windswept and showered with tears.

Falling away, in the late evening rays,
with the sun it was finally slipping,
when it lifted its eyes
took the Shepherd's own hand
that had been there,
from the beginning.

## HUMILITY BROUGHT HOME

From the height of folly,
quite alone,
he views his inclined path,
present once again
amongst the fields
that were his past.

A patchworked quilt beneath
now rises up
to wrap around him,
but he senses little comfort,
from what was once a son's surroundings.

His tattered reputation
brushes freshly growing corn,
and innocence and gaiety
dance round him in the sun.

But a dozen bended backs are stirred,
weathered faces turn to stare,
and a dozen frozen gazes
are giving everything away.

Then another in the distance
throws his honour to the wind,
rushing out with open arms
to wrap his long lost son within.

Nothing stops the father's love;
neither filth nor sordid shame,
compassion hugged, compassion kissed
and then again, again, again.

Brought home to true humility,
he forgets his practiced speech,
now that dreams he'd thought he'd never find,
have been brought within his reach.

# CHAPTER EIGHT

# STAIRWAY TO HEAVEN

*"Blessed are the poor in spirit,*
*for theirs is the kingdom of heaven.*

*Blessed are those who mourn,*
*for they will be comforted.*

*Blessed are the meek,*
*for they will inherit the earth.*

*Blessed are those who hunger and thirst for righteousness,*
*for they will be filled.*

*Blessed are the merciful,*
*for they will be shown mercy.*

*Blessed are the pure in heart,*
*for they will see God.*

*Blessed are the peacemakers,*
*for they will be called sons of God.*

*Blessed are those who are persecuted because of*
*righteousness,*
*for theirs is the kingdom of heaven."*

*Matthew 5: 3-10*

What do you make of the Beattitudes, these 'Beautiful Attitudes' that are at the forefront of Jesus' Mission Statement, the Sermon on the Mount? I used to look at them rather like I looked at my older brother's 'A' level exam papers, when having only just coped with the 11 plus. It wasn't so much a case of *"I don't believe it!"*, although I did have a real problem in seeing how being poor or mourning could be something to relish. It was more that I couldn't believe how I would ever achieve such a state of blessed holiness, any more than being able to one day pass 'A' level physics. To add to my dilemma, I think I soon realised Jesus was not inviting us to 'attempt three of the following', any more than five out of Ten Commandments would qualify you for a place in heaven. Despite sitting through numerous sermons, reading plenty of books, it was more than forty years before I came across something that unlocked these words for me, words I knew in my heart were vitally important.

But first a look at *'Blessed'*, not an easy word to do justice to in translation, any more than *'Shalom'* is simply defined as *'Peace'*. What doesn't help either is the current taste for using the word when confronted by a child being excruciatingly cute as in; *'Ahhh... Bless!'* The Good News Bible tried to modernise it with *'Happy'*, which I used to think dire but now after a bit of mellowing can sort of live with. We do, after all, habitually wish one another *'Happiness'* at every birthday. There is something very important about being happy, not least on your birthday. As a child this tends to be measured by the number of presents and volume of food. Hopefully with age, comes a greater appreciation of those who care enough about you to send you a card, all of which should contribute to us feeling deep down *'Thank God I was born'*. Life is indeed very hard to live, if deep down, we think otherwise. The teaching Jesus offers is his path to finding such inner peace of mind.

But I still have problems with *'Happy'*, as I do with *'Peace'* for Shalom. Both are alright are far as they go, but in my view they don't go far enough. *'Happy'* has at its root *'Hap'* or *'chance'* and I don't believe any of what Jesus is teaching here is down to chance. *'Happy'* is also hijacked too often by those wanting to sell us something, assuring us we will find it in their bottle, by wearing their clothing, driving their car or whatever. It is of course a truism that says 'money can't buy you happiness', even if there are those of you out there who would at least love the chance to one day give it a try.

The difficulty with the Beattitudes comes with thinking we can dive in anywhere. Take number six; *"Blessed are the pure in heart."* Hands up all those who think they are pure in heart. Rather like being convinced your greatest quality is your humility, I suggest that anyone daring to believe such a thing has already failed, due to dishonesty. The unlocking for me came from what Ian Cowie says in his book *'Jesus' Healing Works and Ours'*, where, almost as an aside, he points out that the Beattitudes can be seen as a sequence, a series of steps. They are certainly not some random set of epithets to be picked from by an aspiring mystic. Cowie goes on to explore his approach in terms of Christian healing, a ministry that demands first our attention to the plank in our own eye, before attempting to remove the speck of sawdust from our brother's. In this chapter I would like to develop that idea in relation to healing, given that the Beattitudes apply to every aspect of Christian living.

When it comes to healing we should never assume to know how God does it. A careful look at the New Testament makes it quite clear no two situations are the same. Some demand faith on the part of the one needing healing, in others it is friends having faith on our behalf that counts. Sometimes Jesus asks; *"What do you want me to do for you?"* other times he simply gets on and does it. Our only honest starting point in each case is to admit to God; *"Lord we cannot know what to do. Please give us your wisdom, let us in to your mind."*

In other words we admit to our poverty of understanding. So we can thank God, that in this teaching Jesus begins at the point where he knows all of us to be; *"Blessed are the poor."* The word Jesus uses here is not financial poverty. There is nothing blessed about being destitute, a state that is just as likely to provoke despair and envy rather than piety. Similarly being wealthy is no guarantee of blessing, especially if that wealth is achieved by selfish ambition and accompanied with the fear of losing it. Some versions more helpfully translate it as; *"Blessed are the poor in spirit." (NIV)* or even *"Blessed are those who know their need of God." (J B Phillips)* We shall never take one step up this stairway to heaven, until we first acknowledge that without God we are all paupers. Anyone who arrogantly thinks they don't need God, who even despises the believer for, as they put it 'needing a crutch', will never pass first base. And in ministry terms we may wrongly think we know how God does it and only need call upon him in extremis.

But acknowledging our need of God from the outset, he will welcome our honesty and we shall begin to know what is in his heart. And to love as God loves, is life changing. I remember as a curate going to visit an elderly lady, who for years had attended the Book of Common Prayer Communion each Sunday. Just recently at the altar rail she had received an extraordinary anointing of the Holy Spirit. Being into charismatic renewal at the time, especially through modern worship, I was taught by God a thing or two about not presuming to know how he does things! What struck me about her experience was that ever since, she found herself unable to watch the news without weeping over each report of human suffering. Receiving God's love, we begin to love as he does. Put another way, admitting our need of him, God begins to meet it with his gifts. And every gift God gives comes *'with his love'*.

So we move to the second step; *"Blessed are those who mourn"*. As a rule, if we don't care we don't mourn, though I am mindful of those who at times find it hard to show any outward grief and not through lack of love for the one who has died. But then mourning does not only apply to death. If we love, if we care, we shall, for example, grieve over loss of dignity, peace of mind, purpose in life, health, mobility or whatever. And this may apply to others as well as ourselves. But rather than giving in to despair, our growing faith gives us confidence to believe that all who pass through the experience of loss with God will find; *"they will be comforted"*.

And completing these two first stages, it is not a case of simply ticking off the boxes. Rather, these are two of the foundation stones on which we can then with God continue to build and ascend the stairway. One of the consequences of these first two steps is to find many of our own private agendas are challenged and we are encouraged to surrender them. God needs us to surrender them to what he wants, which is at the heart of; *"Blessed are the meek"*, the third step. The cynic believes 'meekness' to be 'weakness', the believer finds it to be the step by which God will give them extraordinary power, sufficient even to inherit the earth. What wonderful Divine humour at the expense of all who try to achieve it by doing it, Sinatra style, *'My Way'*. Our poverty of spirit is often revealed in the way we resort to our own agendas, mechanisms developed through life to help us cope with situations that challenge us. Many are forged in childhood, self imposed or inflicted by others. They come with seemingly indelible messages such as *I want to be in control* or *I don't want people to see me as I really am*. They may well be the calloused skin that has grown protectively over a painful wound. God in his mercy has ordered things in such a way that, as we proceed up the steps of the Beattitudes, he will begin to heal those hurts and enable us to shed the damaging consequences of them.

At the risk of mixing the metaphors, let me suggest this stairway may also be seen as a ladder, or more precisely a case of 'snakes and ladders'. For to be sure, we have an Enemy intent on frustrating our upward progress. I said earlier that every gift of God comes with his love, not least so that we shall, with that same love be better equipped to exercise the gift to the benefit of others. One of the hazards of Christian healing is that God's gifts can be exercised without his gift of love, as St Paul famously says;

*'If I have the gift of prophecy and can fathom all mysteries and all knowledge and if I have faith that can move mountains but have not love, I am nothing.'*
*(1 Cor 13:2)*

With all respect to Paul, I would dare go further and suggest I could be worse than nothing. I could be a walking disaster area in Christian ministry, that is just as likely to move a mountain and drop it on someone, as if they didn't have enough problems. Slightly less dramatic is the temptation once we think we know how God heals, to then imagine we can control things ourselves and even be tempted to take the credit. But should we find we have slid back down one of those snakes, all is not lost. For through the honest prayer of confession and God's forgiveness he will put us back on track.

Loving with God's love, surrendering our wills to his, we move on to the fourth step; *"Blessed are those who hunger and thirst for righteousness."* We find ourselves sharing his passion for righteousness. And in terms of healing this is not just a hunger for the child in us to simply feel better. The adult is encouraged with maturity to long for 'root and branch' health and wholeness, not only for ourselves and others, but also  for families, communities and nations. By now we are far from playing games, such as wanting to be seen as a healer or a successful Christian. Rather we begin to see others with a much deeper understanding and compassion, as God does and who is himself the embodiment of mercy.

Hence the fifth step; *"Blessed are the merciful."* It is the merciful who find that the mercy we show others will be shown us. And this is not a threat should we fail to, but rather a statement of truth about how God sees all of us. When we understand more of why someone might be a pain to us, we shall find it that much easier to love them with mercy. And seeing ourselves more clearly as God sees us, we should with humility realise the extent to which we might be a pain to others!

95

So to summarise thus far these first five steps. Our honest recognition of needing God is met with his compassion that we can then share with others in distress. This same love encourages us to no longer depend on our own resources but surrender them to God's will and so begin to know his longing for things to be right. All these steps bring us to step six; *"Blessed are pure in heart."* As I suggested at the outset, this step especially reminds us how all this is far less about us and far more about what God is doing in us. On my study wall is a family sampler, made by a distant relative in 1807. It reads:

*Prepare me O my God*
*to stand before Thy face.*
*Thy Spirit must the work perform,*
*for it is all of grace.*

By moving with God up these steps of blessing, one comes to realise by doing so, he is purifying the heart. As our hearts become that much more aligned with his, the mist begins to clear and the prospect is in view so that, *"we shall see God."* In respect of the prayer for healing, this helps us with the constant challenge of knowing whether in each situation we pray for a miracle to cure the problem or the grace to live with it. As we see and know God more clearly, we shall know more confidently how he would have us pray.

And as we continue to ascend these steps another consequence is we become peacemakers and begin to learn how; *"Blessed are the peacemakers."* This is not simply the stuff of international diplomacy, the absence of conflict, but so much more as embodied in the Hebrew word for peace, *Shalom.* This beautiful word embraces health, wholeness, justice, for the individual, families, communities, nations and creation itself. And this peacemaking is like fruit. An apple tree does not have to make a conscious effort to produce apples nor can it produce anything else. When the conditions and the season are right, apples come. When our steps up the Beattitudes are right, our lives in Christ will make peace.

Oh that we could end it there, but we live in a world in such need of healing, a world where, for now, the Enemy remains at large. Jesus is always straight with us. He knows when we dare to ascend the way of blessing, the enemy will do his best to trip us up. As we approach the eighth and final step, Jesus prepares us to expect the Enemy's concerted attention through the familiar tactic of persecution. It may take many forms and come from various quarters. But we are to keep our eyes on Jesus and his life changing teaching, words that defy worldly wisdom, as do all the Beattitudes for; *"Blessed are you if you are persecuted for doing right."* For his promise to us is that as we approach the top step; *"Rejoice and be glad, for great is your reward in heaven."*

POSTSCRIPT

Being the perfect teacher that he is, Jesus never calls us to do something he would not do himself. Another way to get deeper into the Beattitudes is to reflect on the way Jesus himself lives them out in his own earthly life. There is of course no sense in which Christ has to progress toward holiness. Yet his life and death clearly need to  follow the route ordained by his Father, a route he has to choose in obedience, above all in Gethsemane *"Yet not as I will but as you will" (Matt 26:39)* I offer some verses and examples but you may like to study the Beattitudes again and think of others.

*"Blessed are those who know their need of God."* Jesus is of course the Son of God, yet as the son of the Father he frequently expresses his total dependence on him as in; *"I tell you the truth, the Son can do nothing by himself." (John 5:19)*
*"Blessed are those who mourn"* Of all the verses in the New Testament there are few more poignant than the shortest one,

when we read that on hearing of the death of his dear friend Lazarus *"Jesus wept" (John 11:35)*

*"Blessed are the meek"* Jesus says of himself *"Take my yoke upon you and learn from me, for I am gentle (meek) and humble in heart."* Of all people, Jesus alone has complete justification in making this claim for himself.

*"Blessed are those who hunger and thirst for righteousness."* The whole of his life is marked by a passion for righteousness and perhaps no more vividly than when driving out of the Temple the corrupt traders and moneychangers. (Matthew 21:12f)

*"Blessed are the merciful."* As with his righteousness, the mercy of Jesus is shown time and again in his life, perhaps none more so than the way in which he dealt with the woman taken in adultery (John 8:1-11)

*"Blessed are the pure in heart."* Unlike us, there was never a time when Jesus heart was not pure, having been born without sin, yet for our salvation *"God made him who had no sin to be sin for us."(2 Cor 5:21)* The moment came as he was dying, when becoming sin for us, for the first time his intimate communion with the Father was severed and from his perspective on the cross he could no longer see God and so cried: *"My God, my God, why have you forsaken me?" (Matthew 27:46)*

*"Blessed are the peacemakers."* Paul writes to the Ephesians of Jesus destroying the wall of hostility, *"for he himself is our peace." (Eph 2:14)*

*"Blessed are those who are persecuted because of righteousness."* From his rejection at Nazareth (Luke 4:14 f) to the cross itself, Jesus experiences persecution for daring to challenge every denial of righteousness.

QUESTIONS

1. What do you think are the characteristics of a life that does not believe it needs God and one that does?

2. What other agendas do you think we might adopt and resort to in life?

3. Have you ever thought of the Beattitudes as being a sequence?

4. What are the marks of a peacemaker?

5. When we see God, what do we see?


POEMS

Two poems again this time. *Holy Fire* was written in the eighties, a time when we were experiencing a movement of the Holy Spirit in the church. At its heart are three principles that I see rooted in the Beattitudes: Our own hearts remaining cold and impoverished until we acknowledge our need of God, his love to us inspiring our love for others and it all happening as a process, as we are called to grow up and into the likeness of Christ.

The other, *Meditating on a Cactus* is a little lighter. My plant collection began many years ago with a single cactus from a jumble sale, priced sixpence. I've always found them fascinating and enjoyed learning how these extraordinary plants have adapted to cope with some of the harshest conditions on earth. Though we too may adapt as a way of coping, I see Jesus, through the Beattitudes giving us a way to let him reverse the process, if need be, and appreciate the potential inside even some of the most hostile of exteriors. The idea of meditating on a cactus reminds us he never said it would be comfortable!

## HOLY FIRE

Kindle in each parchment heart,
tinder dry, the Holy Spark;
blow your breath and draw the flame
illuminate our deepest shame,
burn within and light without,
make us cry the angry shout.

Cry for tender loving wishes,
warm embrace and gentle kisses,
cry for eyes to run with tears,
desert dry these many years;
cry for time a pain to share,
to be around and simply care.

Then from stony faces see
the callous of complacency,
shed in layers with each new action;
God at work in Christ's compassion.

## MEDITATING ON A CACTUS

Enough faith to follow
is all I should ask now,
to find in the desert
a way I can grow,
to see as benevolent
these testing extremes,
the soul shivering dark night
and sight blinding sun.

But should I grow cactus like,
tactically fending off contact,
through spine upon spike
in a tightly knit mask,
then open the green folds,
turned in on themselves,
as you see the inside,
as no one else can;
the bud of a flower
in time yet to be,
a kernel of hope
for a glory to come.

# THE WIDOW'S OFFERING - GIVING IT ALL
## LUKE 20:45-47, 21:1-4

*"As he looked up, Jesus saw the rich putting their gifts into the temple treasury. He also saw a poor widow put in two very small copper coins. 'I tell you the truth', he said 'this poor widow has put in more than all the others. All these people gave their gifts out of their wealth; but she out of her poverty put in all she had lo live on.'" Luke 21 1-4*

Some years ago a couple I knew attended church regularly, together with their grown up daughter, who at the time had a young child of her own. They were a devoted Christian family, but the daughter sadly suffered at times with a troubled mind. On one occasion they were in church together and this passage from Luke was read out. I don't know whether it was preached on in a particular way, but when it came to taking up the collection, the daughter emptied her purse into the plate. Her parents were dismayed, for they well knew how she struggled to make ends meet but they were also at a loss to know what to say. Was she not simply doing what the Bible was telling her to? In which case part of them couldn't help rejoicing that she was wanting to live by faith. Either way, the upshot was her parents had to pay the bills for her, until the next benefit arrived.

This event brought to a head something that had long bothered me about this story from Luke. In fact, the couple came to me asking what I thought about it all. I confess to having no simple answer at the time but remember admitting this was a passage

I had always been uncomfortable with. I went on to say I found it hard to believe Jesus was saying the poorest must give away even what little they have to live on. But then again, living by faith does not depend on how much or how little you have. If God wants us to put everything we have at his disposal, how much we have is immaterial.

I began to wonder if my problem was not so much with what Jesus was saying than with what we did with it. So often this passage is called upon by the Church when wanting to raise funds. That particular use of this Scripture bothers me more than anything, not least having attended many Christian events where I've felt inordinate pressure was exerted on those present to 'give sacrificially'. And there cannot in my view be any worse example of this, than some of those TV evangelists who seem prepared to go to any lengths to extract donations from their audiences. One such individual wrote to a widow in a nursing home asking for $200, saying if she didn't have it, she should borrow it. He claimed God had told him to write the letter. Unfortunately the woman had been dead for three months. Possibly heaven was slow in updating their records, but I think not. What possibly makes the problem unique to our age are the huge audiences that can be reached by the media and the temptation to extract huge amounts from them.

As I said in the opening story, there was no suggestion the preacher at that particular service had used any such coercion. For all I know he may not have even referred to the story of the widow's offering. What it does highlight though is how little we may know of the congregation or audience, and how there may well be those present who are susceptible to irrational actions by reason of their state of mind.

In exploring this delicate matter I plan to share some of the conclusions I have drawn over the years, not least when, as a church leader, I had at least some of the responsibility for finances. But before we do that, let's return to this specific Scripture. Once again I have to admit that years of not understanding or even misunderstanding were ended recently when my son came back from Spring Harvest. At this large Christian teaching event he had listened to a revealing exposition of this passage given by a Baptist pastor. The speaker took them back to the previous verses at the end of chapter twenty. Bear in mind there were originally no chapters and verses so you have to read the surrounding text carefully to get the full picture. What is quite apparent is that the whole of chapter twenty and probably all of twenty one takes place at the same time in the Temple, where Jesus is teaching. There can be no doubt the incident with the widow happened immediately after Jesus had been speaking these words; *"While all the people were listening, Jesus said to his disciples, 'Beware of the teachers of the law. They like to walk around in flowing robes and love to be greeted in the market places and have the most important seats in the synagogues and the places of honour at banquets. They devour widows' houses and for a show make lengthy prayers. Such men will be punished most severely.'"*

Look carefully at that curious phrase *"they devour widows' houses"*. Having just heard they like the best places at banquets, one cannot help but sit up and take notice at this comical association of ideas. Of course the people listening knew the teachers of the law were not into eating masonry! But this vivid image must have had everyone highly attentive for what was about to happen. They would have known very well what Jesus was talking about. There were unscrupulous religious leaders then, as in any generation, who used their position and power to get rich at the expense of fellow believers. Long before the days of social security, if a woman lost her husband she was in danger of becoming destitute. He may well have had in mind these verses from Isaiah; *"Woe to those who make unjust laws, to those who issue oppressive decrees, to deprive the poor of their rights and withhold justice from the oppressed of my people, making widows their prey and robbing the fatherless." (Is 10:12)* In a world ruled by men, widows were not allowed to own property or handle any money their dead husbands may have left them, so it became the role of the Scribes, teachers of the law, to appoint someone to do this for them. However by the time of Jesus, the Scribes were habitually defrauding these most vulnerable of people, leaving them impoverished and in despair. And of course widows were not necessarily elderly. Some would be young, with children to care for. Such exploitation by the religious leaders drew the wrath of Jesus as it did when he turned over the tables and expelled the corrupt traders and money changers. Take note, this dramatic event has happened very recently and would still be fresh in everyone's mind.

Take note also the beginning of chapter twenty one reads; *"As he looked up"* Jesus the rabbi is sitting down as he teaches, those listening are standing; the opposite of what we are used to. I'm not suggesting Jesus could in some way have organised what then happens but I wouldn't put it past his Father! There in front of them all were the people putting their gifts into the collecting vessels. These would have been large metallic containers, ideal for pouring a bag full of coins into if you wanted everyone to know how generous you were being. On the other hand, two tiny copper coins would have hardly made any noise at all.

What I was suddenly made to realise was perhaps I'd got it wrong all along, not least because others had presumably taught it wrong all along. Far from using the occasion to commend the widow's sacrificial generosity, and thereby suggest all poor people should do the same, Jesus could also be saying; *"Look at that! There you have a perfect example of what I'm talking about. On the one hand are those wealthy people making a show of giving what has cost them little. On the other is a poor widow who has been exploited by the religious teachers into giving them all she had to live on."*

As far as I can see, there are no other interpretations but these two. For my money I know which one I am ready to go with. And those of us Church leaders who have responsibility for guiding people how they should give, think long and hard about what Jesus is saying, not least to those who may be tempted to abuse their position  and to whom he says you *"will be punished most severely"*. All of that I realise may make it even harder to persuade someone to take on the job of Church Treasurer! So all the more reason to consider just what did Jesus mean when he talked about them being punished most severely? Here we have to look especially to the surrounding text and remember that Jesus is thinking specifically of the Scribes of his time. These were self appointed religious teachers, who by now had become universally corrupt, being more interested in amassing their own wealth than caring about the poor. Part of this corruption, as we have already mentioned was the abuse of Temple trade by the money changers and sellers of sacrificial doves. To put it simply the whole system was rotten and the severe punishment they were to expect was then set out very clearly as the narrative continues; *"Some of his disciples were remarking about how the Temple was adorned with beautiful stones and with gifts dedicated to God. But Jesus said, 'As for what you see here, the time will come when not one stone will be left on another, every one of them will be thrown down.'" (Luke 21: 5-6)* It seems the disciples have simply not been listening. They appear to be marvelling at the lavishly decorated Temple, when Jesus has just pointed out that all that wealth is too often at the expense of those who can least afford it. And this whole edifice both harbours and is maintained by a corrupt system, but not for much longer. For what Jesus predicted would happen in less than forty years time, in AD 70. The Temple and its system were raised to the ground by the Romans and to date they have never been restored. So with a sigh of relief I believe we can put to one side the prospect of severe punishment for getting it wrong. And now let me explore a little further this whole area of giving, as much in terms of what I have personally found helpful over the years.

As a starting point we will take *'The Widow's Offerring'* but not as a justification for using coercion, manipulation or any other exploitation to extract money from people wrongly. To be honest this principle is not just for Church leaders, but for any one, not least the great majority of Christians who have to live and work in the world. It is after all at the heart of much commerce to use advertisements to persuade people to buy what they didn't think they needed. I noticed the other day, on my rotary mower the word *'Warning'* in four languages, the French being *'Avertissement'*. Perhaps if we all appreciated where the word comes from we might be a little less gullible in believing what they tell us! But to be serious, I believe the way we deal with one another financially is a huge field in which to exercise the Kingdom principles of *'The Sower'* and *'The Broad and Narrow Way.'* If you have dived into the book at this point, I recommend you read Chapters Two and Three to get my point!

When it comes to giving, someone once said to me *'You can't out-give God'*. An early example of that was when we first married and joined up with two other couples in a small prayer group. Both of them followed the principle of tithing, giving away a tenth of all their income. Like many, I suspect, my first introduction to Christian giving was the sixpence mum gave me to put in the collection when I went to Sunday School. The whole experience was traumatic. Assuming I didn't lose it on the way to church, I would put it carefully on the pew in front of me as soon as I arrived. Long before they came round with the bags, it would inevitably fall on the floor at least once. And when I saw the sidesmen making their way toward me I would be filled with worry in case I fluffed it when my turn came. Given that the money came out of mum's purse and not my pocket money, all in all it was not much of a preparation for when our friends suggested we tried tithing. To be fair they were not coercive, but only shared their own experience, that as they had found the courage to be generous with God, somehow what remained seemed to go so much further. But more importantly, they found the joy of being able to make meaningful gifts to individuals and causes that they especially cared about.

Some suggest at least the majority of our gifts should go directly to our own church, trusting those in charge will use it in accordance with God's will. I think there's a lot to be said for that, though it could mean we're largely giving to what we ourselves benefit from. For that reason and others, I have always felt better when any church has a generous approach to supporting causes beyond themselves. All this I would say is a matter for each of us to decide, as indeed with tithing itself which I appreciate some believe to be rather too legalistic. They would say that under the new covenant, God enables us to live in greater freedom, looking to the Holy Spirit rather than the rule of law. What I did find helpful was to learn that in Jewish thinking, by giving ten per cent, God then consecrated the ninety per cent we retained. In any event, my wife and I decided to give it a go and I can only say time and again we have since proved what others had said; *'You can't out-give God'.*

Another principle of tithing is that this is only the starting point and in the Old Testament we read of all kinds of other offerings. Here I may seem to go full circle, for I have to admit there may be times when God calls us to be utterly generous, even to the point of giving everything we have. The testimonies of many Christian lives bear witness to this and you could be wondering whether the traditional teaching on *The Widow's Offering* is not right after all. Here I believe we come to the nub of it all, that is how to know the right thing to do in each situation. The answer must come from our listening to the Holy Spirit, whom Jesus and the Father have given us *"to guide us into all truth" (John 16:13)* Thanks to Jesus, we have the way to live a life of faith, directed not by the written word alone but by the same Spirit of God that inspired its writing in the first place.

As with all Scripture, I believe if approached with sincerity, God will interpret it to us in our own situation and in our own day, not least in the matter of giving. He never intended our giving should be merely out of a sense of duty, even less as obeying the rules, for fear of the consequences of not doing so.

Rather he desires that living in partnership with him we can be confident to know day by day what he would have us do as co workers with him in the Kingdom. Such a wonderful prospect should fill us with excitement and eagerness, for truly his word says; *"God loves a cheerful giver." (2 Cor: 9:7)*

QUESTIONS

1. What do think the story of 'The Widow's Offering' is saying about giving?

2. Do you think a Christian should tithe?

3. If you make a donation, how do you decide where to give and what you give?

4. If you had to work in a job where you were expected to do something you didn't think was right, how would you handle it?

5. Do you think you are influenced by advertisements?

N.B. In using these questions in a group, I would not expect for one minute that anyone should reveal the actual amounts of what they give, unless you know one another very well!

POEM

Not all the Scribes and Pharisees were to come under condemnation from Jesus.
There was one in particular who, together with another prominent citizen, gave it all up, even though they had yet to see Jesus rise from the dead.

*"Now there was a man of the Pharisees named Nicodemus, a member of the ruling Jewish Council. He came to Jesus at night." (John 3:1-2)*

*"Later, Joseph of Arimathea asked Pilate for the body of Jesus... he came and took the body accompanied by Nicodemus." (John 19:38-42)*

## NICODEMUS AND JOSEPH

In dead of night
he creeps from city shadows,
a hooded face
in fear and fascination;
a torturous route,
a cross road
and a path with many options,
moth-like drawn to light
that seeps beneath a bolted door.

A pounding heart
he bears on softened footsteps,
in rapid breaths
he seeks out watching eyes,
a swimming head,
where deep inside
opposing voices rise
in urgent whispers;
standing at the door
he stops and knocks.

Opening
the warmth and light flood over him,
sweet smells of home
and comfort of good company;
a single step,
a question mark,
the answer leaves him wondering,
yet embraced by perfect Love
there is conception;
and so returns to home,
that never feels like home again.

In light of day
he steps from crowded alleys,
a weeping face
in fixed determination,
a laboured route,
a cross road
and a path that had no option;
all his hope is still - born,
aborted expectations,
yet still he comes in hope
he will find home again.


Beneath the cross
they stoop in stunned emotion,
with offered hands
to take the broken Christ,
as one in love
they lift their God between them,
their clothing stained with red,
identified,
their own positions,
crucified,
blood brothers born
in truth
again.

# CHAPTER TEN
# BORN IN A PUB?

My family know there are certain things about Christmas that really get me going, the worst of them having to listen to carols in June. Writing this then, as we approach Easter I need to steel myself, not least as it causes me to remember a few years ago hearing someone on the local radio who loved Christmas so much he had it every day of the year. Every day he'd wrap himself some presents which he'd then carefully open, prepare a turkey dinner, put on the carols and sit down to watch the Queen. What's even more extraordinary, he was still married! If that has the same effect on your stomach as it does mine, my apologies if you are reading this while sitting on the beach in high summer, unless of course you're in Australia.

There is so much about the traditional Christmas I find hard to believe, from Santa upwards. But in my heart I know the story to be profoundly true, a real historical event, no less than the birth on earth of the Son of God. Yet I cannot help but keep coming back to the bits that worry me, like a dog with a bone. In fact I am reminded of a dog we used to have in the family. When going for a walk in the country, he was off into every patch of undergrowth in search of treasures, mostly rabbits. We would have thought him unwell and it all rather sad if he'd only wanted to walk placidly at our side. But regularly he would break off from his quest and come bounding back, give us a quick sniff to reassure himself we were still there and then return to the chase. So rather than the Easter bunny, this is my version of a Christmas rabbit hunt, based on things I've picked up over the years, not least through those who have introduced me to the value of exploring our Jewish roots. But however far I may wander into the undergrowth in my eagerness, rest assured I shall regularly return to touch base with the most important aspects of this wonderful story, that I know will reassuringly always be there for us.

Let's start with the date, December 25th, which is highly unlikely to be the right one, not least because we know it had for long been the date of a midwinter pagan festival. More likely it was a shrewd move on the part of the first Christians to choose that date, as everyone was already geared up to having a party at that time. All they had to do was change one letter in order to worship the Son rather than the sun! Another argument suggests that the shepherds would not have been out in the fields in midwinter, not for their sake but for the sake of the sheep. One of the gems I was delighted to discover, was that Bethlehem was where the lambs for the Passover festival were raised. Since the lambs for sacrifice had to be perfect and without blemish they would have been safely tucked away in barns during the winter months. I never fail to marvel at the precision with which God orders events, like a skilled carpenter who delights in making joints that fit perfectly. How perfect then that the Lamb of God should be born in the same place as all the other sacrificial lambs. And while on the subject, are you aware what Bethlehem means? It comes from *Beit Lehem*, the Hebrew name for 'House of Bread.' So for good measure, the Bread of Life is born in the House of Bread. Great, I love it!

But if not 25th December, when? I realise we are in the realms of conjecture, but on the basis that God is ordering so much when it comes to the birth of his Son, I can't help thinking the date would matter a lot to him. In fact not so much the date, as what was already happening at the time. The Bible tells us that Bethlehem was full to overflowing and there was *"no room at the inn"*. The assumption is that it was full because of the census the Romans had called for. It's true there would have been extra people come back to register, but nothing like the number there would have been on any one of three other occasions each year. Long ago, God had instructed that every man in Israel fit to travel should attend Jerusalem for three major annual festivals. Bethlehem being just a couple of miles from Jerusalem was a popular place for the vast crowds of people to stay. The festivals were Passover in Spring, Pentecost in late Spring and Tabernacles in the Autumn. If that was the cause of the shortage of rooms, it could mean then that Jesus was born either at Passover or Pentecost. But following the thought of God ordering events, is it not much neater that the Lamb of God should die and rise at Passover, the Holy Spirit should come at Pentecost and that the birth take place at the Feast of Tabernacles?

God had ordained Tabernacles for the people to recall the time when they were in the Wilderness, an unfamiliar and hostile place. They were to build temporary shelters to live in, to remind them that, despite the transience of this life, God was with them. It also encouraged them to look forward to the time when God would bring them into the Promised Land and they would enjoy an even closer relationship with him. St John in the opening of his gospel tells how; *"The Word became flesh and made his dwelling among us." (1:14)* What he actually writes is; *"The Word became flesh and tabernacled among us."* Could it be that John, who otherwise has nothing to say about the practicalities of Jesus' birth, gives us a sign, by using the word 'tabernacle'? Either way, I still maintain of all the three major Jewish Festivals, Tabernacles best illuminates what Christmas is all about. By taking on our flesh, God was not only showing he was very much with us, but also for love of us he was subjecting himself to all the frailties of being human.

Another puzzle to me has always been the star. I know we must be careful not to rely on carols for our theology. When it comes to *'We three Kings'*, we know they were not kings but magi and whilst they brought three gifts, there could have been any number of donors and the Bible certainly doesn't tell us their names. But more important is the star. Some choose to see the whole event as mythical but I am not comfortable with that. I am satisfied this was a real event, that they saw something and this something led them to the infant. Every year people speculate about the convergence of stars, supernova, comets and every other kind of astronomical event. But given how any of these would have been millions of miles away, I don't see how they could be over a precise location on the earth's surface.

Throughout the Old Testament are times when God's presence is marked by what in Hebrew is called the *Shekinah*. It is a mysterious phenomenon usually involving light and often translated as his *Glory*. We see it in the Wilderness guiding the people at night and there were times when it was to be seen in the Temple, as visual evidence of God's presence. My only problem is how could you have some supernatural light hovering over the place in Bethlehem where Jesus was, without far more than a few shepherds and magi being attracted to it? If you had been living nearby, wouldn't you have been tempted to go and knock on the door? Having said that, I realise there is good evidence that the magi came anything up to two years later and not at the same time as the shepherds, in which case one then wonders how the shepherds knew where to go. Here I am going to stick my neck out and suggest not only was it the Shekinah Glory of God but as on other occasions, only those God intended were able to see it. In I Kings 6:17 we read of Elijah asking God to open Elisha's eyes to see the celestial army that surrounded them. In the New Testament, when Saul is met by the ascended Jesus on the road to Damascus he is surrounded by light. Those with him heard the sound but saw nothing. (Acts 9: 3,7) After all, the last thing Mary and Joseph needed was an endless stream of sightseers, especially if they included Herod's men.

And so to my main point and the title of this chapter. Was Jesus born in a pub, or rather a stable round the back of a pub? I said we need to take care not to base our theology on carols, similarly I suggest beware of Nativity plays! I know everyone has to have a part and fortunately there is no biblical limit to the number of angels and shepherds, but the ubiquitous appearance of the innkeeper really takes the biscuit! Dressed in his apron, from having just changed the barrels and with pint mug in hand, it's no wonder we swallow this idea that Jesus was born in a pub. We can trace the problem back to the translators of the King James Bible. They read in the Greek that Mary had to give birth among the animals because there was no room in the place where anyone with any decency would have let her stay, even if it meant giving up their own bed. The word they chose to use, 'inn' was what they thought best at the time and it seems to have stuck. But the word can also be translated as 'living quarters'. Typical of Mediterranean houses, you would have the living quarters on the first floor, usually in the form of wide balconies with the animals stabled on the ground floor. Your animals were some of your most precious possessions and the last place you would put them was round the back in a separate shed from which they might escape or be stolen. The added bonus is that they provided a useful source of central heating on cold nights. With your living quarters on a balcony, you could easily keep an eye and an ear on them.

If this interpretation is right, it meant Mary had to join the animals on the ground floor to give birth and that is extraordinary, not least in a land that values hospitality so highly. But bear in mind she fell pregnant whilst unmarried, an offence normally punished by stoning to death or at least ostracism. A couple of years ago, the BBC ran an excellent series at Christmas about this story. Gritty and realistic they had Joseph knocking on the door of a relative in Bethlehem, which is of course where he would have naturally gone, not the local pub, had there been one. In the programme they open the door, see Joseph and are delighted. But then they see Mary, heavy with child and their attitude changes; *'There's room for you, but not her.'* I know it's not specifically in the text, but let me suggest another possibility. Could it be that Joseph, in desperation finally got them to agree to let her stay on the ground floor, with the animals? Otherwise can you imagine a situation where a relative about to give birth calls on you and you slam the door in their face, whatever you may think of them? To my mind this interpretation of events would say something even more profound about the birth of Jesus than our usual telling of the story allows. It says to me that Jesus is born in the house of David, right in the heart of it, as God's word always said he would be. But to reveal God's humility and our hardened hearts, he is denied even the most basic of comfort and has to enter the house at the lowest level possible. Just as Jesus was to be brought up in Nazareth, a place from which, in popular thought; *"nothing of any good can come" (John 1:46)*, God is, through his Incarnation, challenging all our prejudices. If we are to ever recognise the Messiah for who he truly is, we dare not rely on worldly wisdom, for as with the star, the truth will be rendered invisible to us.

Before we put the decorations away and move on to the next chapter, let's spare a thought for Mary, mother of our Lord and for that matter for Joseph. Soon after the birth, they were to hear prophetically that a sword would pierce her soul (Luke 2:35). I'd always imagined that referred to when she would see her son being crucified, but I wonder now whether she didn't begin to feel the point of it the moment she said 'yes' to God. There's no evidence that any but a few of those nearest to her realised the truth. Many of those she had to live alongside in Nazareth would presumably always have seen her as disgraceful. One can imagine some going so far as to refer to her as *'that slut who got pregnant out of wedlock'*. Forgive me if that shocks you but I can't help feeling we sanitise this story far too much. In just the same way, we seek to take the edge off the crucifixion. Mel Gibson's film *The Passion of the Christ* is not one I think I could watch again, but I applaud its dreadful reality. And without putting too fine a point on it, Jesus would not have been afforded a discreet loin cloth. Crucifixion was intended to shock the onlookers and shame the victim. But even that bit of realism, I seem to remember, the film shied away from, just as every example of religious art does too.

Returning to Nazareth from Egypt, I am convinced they would have found that gossips have sharp tongues and long memories and I truly believe the whole family, including Jesus would have lived under that cloud for many years.

To return to Bethlehem, what lengths we go to in trying to tidy up the stable. On the basis of the cards and carols, anyone would have thought they'd got an upgrade. When I first took on a parish, in early December I had five tons of well rotted farm yard manure dropped in the front drive of the Vicarage. Not as some thought to deter carol singers but as part of my grand designs for the garden. I did decorate it with a sprig of holly, giving the nice effect of a large Christmas pudding. Sat in my study, seeking inspiration for my first Midnight Mass sermon, my eyes fell on the heap. So on Christmas Eve I took a large bucket of it up into the pulpit, much to the consternation of the choir beneath. My aim was to try and cut through the tinsel and get back to what it would actually have been like on that first Christmas. I wondered too how I might have felt when taking my wife to Sevenoaks Maternity Unit for the birth of our first son only to be told; *'Sorry we're full. Try the local farm, they've got some nice dry barns'.* Whether the stable was on the ground floor, round the back of the pub or the back of beyond, what we did to Mary and Joseph was nothing short of disgraceful. I say 'we' advisedly because for too long the Church pressed the point that the Jews were cursed for rejecting the Messiah, giving them the name 'God Killers'. With such an attitude, there are sadly too few more steps to the gates of Belsen. The fact that most of us at the time failed to recognise the Saviour coming among us, is in some sense immaterial. For we repeatedly make the same mistake in every generation, including our own. I remind you of what some of us will hear Jesus say as we all finally stand before him on the Day of Judgement; ***"For I was hungry and you gave me nothing to eat, I was thirsty and you gave me nothing to drink, I was a stranger and you did not invite me in, I needed clothes and you did not cloth***

***me, I was sick and in prison and you did not look after me.*** *(Matthew 25:42-43)*

Given that Mary's immediate need was none of these, I'm sure you will appreciate that Jesus' list is not definitive, but is meant to illustrate every situation in which we may or not choose to show mercy. That is also I suggest what Christmas is all about, as is the poem with which I close this Chapter, *Refuse Madonna*. I wrote it many years ago, inflamed by seeing on television a young South American girl with a baby under her arm scavenging for food on the edge of a rubbish tip, on the outskirts of a big city.

But to return for a moment to Mary herself, there is an extraordinary passage in Mark; ***"Then Jesus entered a house and again a crowd gathered, so that he and his disciples were not even able to eat. When his family heard about this they went to take charge of him, for they said 'He is out of his mind'."*** *(Mark 3:20)* I refer you to what I said in Chapter Four about Mark giving us the grittiest of the Gospels, for he alone refers to this disturbing event, which the other three writers choose to omit. Who exactly is the 'family'? Did it include Mary, his mother? After all that she had been through, had she been brought to the point of believing that her son was out of his mind? Even if it was only other family members that thought like this, how much pain could that have caused Mary, when they called into question the state of Jesus' mind? All in all this tends to bring out the bit of catholic in me, which I would commend to any from another tradition that may feel uncomfortable about dwelling too much on Mary. In my other book, *The Holy Caterpillar* I expressed my sincerest thanks to her, for going through all that for us. I just want to say once again, amen to that.

## REFUSE MADONNA

See him lying
in a bed of sores,
powerless in poverty,
while overhead a fighter roars,
declares with pride its territory
and from its tail sprays out its waste
upon the child and mother.

A mother picking
what she can,
from the discharge of the city,
this rotten waste of modern man,
tipped out to soil humanity,
teetering on the edge of life,
this blessed scavenger.

Pity the Madonna and her child
Oh yes, for shame;
but save your greatest pity
for the one who bears the blame;
the one whose fortune rots in banks,
whose taxes go for guns and tanks,
whose luxury and expensive taste
keep them living on his waste.

Who dares to point a finger
at the heavens we're polluting,
and shout at God accusingly,
"Why, oh why, the suffering?"

POSTSCRIPT

At the outset I suggested we could confidently explore some of the uncertain aspects of the Christmas story, whilst remaining sure of the core truths that really mattered. I confess to not always thinking quite that way. Some years ago I came across a pamphlet that offered numerous reasons why 'real' Christians should have nothing to do with the traditional Christmas. There was everything from mistletoe and holly being pagan, to santa being an anagram of satan! I was initially intrigued and almost persuaded to suggest to the congregation we abandon 25th December, Christmas trees and all the rest and instead go for something far more biblical around the time of Tabernacles. Thankfully commonsense prevailed, not just for the sake of tradition but I do believe God to be very understanding. I cannot imagine him closing his ears to our worship on 25th December, simply because we may have got the date wrong. I'm reminded too of a story I heard told by the Christian author and speaker Adrian Plass. Some years back when his children were young, he had to spend much time on the road and on one occasion booked into a hotel feeling especially sorry for himself, not least because it was his birthday. As he sat in the dreary room, he opened an envelope. It was from his little daughter, who had drawn him a picture with the message *"Love you Daddy, missing you lots. Happy Birthday"*. The picture was meant to be of him, but the eyes were crooked, the mouth out of all proportion and his hair completely the wrong colour. Adrian said how when he got home he said to his daughter: *"How dare you misrepresent me like that! Don't even think of doing it again until you've learnt how to draw properly."* For a moment there was an embarrassed silence in the audience until he said, *"Only joking"*.

I do suspect God is very used to having us talk about him and worship him with much to be desired, when it comes to accuracy. It's no excuse for carelessness where we do know better, but on the other hand, he is I am sure far more interested in the sincerity of what we offer. So come on, let's deck the halls with boughs of holly (in due season) if it brings us joy and helps us worship him in spirit and in truth.


QUESTIONS

1. Would you encourage your children to believe in Santa Claus?

2. What do you think the star was?

3. What's the best thing about Christmas for you?

4. Do you believe Jesus was born in a stable at the back of a pub? Would it matter if he wasn't?

5. Is there anything we could do about the popular way of celebrating Christmas to make more of its true meaning?

6. What do you think about celebrating Christmas at the Feast of Tabernacles, even as a 'one off'?

# CHAPTER ELEVEN

# THE DAY OF PENTECOST

*"When the day of Pentecost came, they were all together in one place. Suddenly a sound like the blowing of a violent wind came from heaven and filled the whole house where they were sitting." Acts 2: 1-2*

Here is a simple question. Where were the disciples on the day of Pentecost? For many years I would not have hesitated to answer *"In the upper room"* and I have a strong suspicion many of you reading this would say the same. Perhaps we take a cue from the previous chapter of Acts that describes an earlier occasion when they met the risen Jesus and how *"they went upstairs to the room where they were staying." (Acts 1:13)* It certainly looks like this was the disciples' base, all the time they were still in Jerusalem. It could be it was a different upstairs room to the one in which Jesus had kept Passover, before the crucifixion. One might ask, does it really matter? It was obviously some house or other, surely what happened there is more important. In this chapter I want to suggest where they were and what they were doing matters a great deal also.

I have another question. Do you find any of the three persons of the Trinity; Father, Son and Holy Spirit to be especially enigmatic? Again, I know how I would have answered that for many years. I am sure I am not alone as a Christian in having found the Holy Spirit by far the most difficult to comprehend. As I grew up, the Father was the awesome power behind all creation, Jesus I could read about in the Gospels but who or what on earth is the Holy Spirit? The reasons for this in my case were,

I am sure, many and varied but much of the uncertainty was clarified for me through the charismatic movement. From the late sixties on, there was something remarkable happening in the Church in this country and others. Sometimes controversial, nonetheless many Christians undeniably found their life of faith taking on a new and more vital dimension, as we encountered the Holy Spirit. And up to fifty years on, the fruit of what God was doing then is still to be seen.

This was an experience I was privileged to share in and yet through it all something still niggled. The more I thought about the day of Pentecost and the way it has been often pictured, the greater the voice within was muttering; *"I don't believe it!"* It wasn't that I didn't believe the Holy Spirit came upon the disciples, or that they became supernaturally able to communicate in languages they had not previously known. And whether these are languages of earth or of heaven, I am now content to believe they can be either. My concern was with what may seem a very prosaic issue. How on earth did they all fit into that upper room? Read the account right through and you'll find that; *"...about three thousand were added to their number that day (Acts 2:41)* Given that far from everyone present signed up that day, this was some gathering. Back in my youth I remember a party in an upstairs flat in Clapham that certainly felt like such an occasion, but in reality it was a fraction of the size.

I also remember seeing this scene depicted in a film. Peter goes to the window and out onto a balcony and with a kind of papal touch addresses the throng down below. Even before we first visited old Jerusalem back in the eighties, I'd seen enough photographs to know you would be hard pressed to get a crowd of three hundred into any of those narrow streets, let alone three thousand plus.

Let me cut to the chase. I am convinced there is only one place they could possibly have been. Indeed as the conscientious Jews that they were, they were simply obeying what God had commanded them to do many centuries before, that every able bodied man in Israel was to appear before him in Jerusalem three times a year at the Feasts of Tabernacles, Passover and Pentecost. (Deuteronomy 16:16) And by the time of Jesus, the only place to do that was in the Temple. It would not have crossed their mind to be anywhere else. Some of us Christians may take quite lightly an obligation to be in church for the major festivals, but that was not the case with the Jews of Jesus' day and certainly not those he had been training for the past three years. One remembers too that less than forty days ago, cross examined by the high priest, Jesus replied; *"I always taught in synagogues or at the Temple, where all the Jews come together." (John 18:20)* And after the ascension, Luke records the disciples *"stayed continually at the Temple praising God" (34:53)* There is no evidence before or after the resurrection of this being changed during the days leading up to Pentecost.

I know that Pentecost is now sometimes referred to as *'The Birthday of the Church'* but back then at nine o'clock in the morning it was still going through labour. The event they would all have naturally been participating in was the Feast of Pentecost that centred on the Temple. What actually took place each year and largely still does for Jews, is very relevant to what was about to happen. But more about that shortly.

*"But hold on"* do I hear someone say? *"doesn't the Bible say they were sitting in the house?"* Fair point, only *'house'* can also be translated as *'Temple'*, just as we might refer to a church as *'the house of God'*. More to the point, when Jesus cleanses the Temple he says; *"It is written 'My house will be called a house of prayer', but you are making into a 'den of robbers'". (Matt 21:13)* Even today if you were to ask a Jerusalem taxi driver to take you to the Temple Mount and you spoke Hebrew, you would say *'Har Ha-Bayit'* which is literally *'Mountain of the House'*. What is curious, is that our Bibles invariably translate this as *'house'* without even a footnote pointing out that it could also mean *'Temple'*. We also need

to appreciate that in Jewish parlance, to describe someone as *'sitting in the house'* is a colloquial way of saying they were simply *'in the house.'*

But first let's return to that earlier occasion when the risen Lord Jesus was eating with the disciples (Acts 1:4-8) and told them to stay in the city for *"you will receive power when the Holy Spirit comes on you"*. As Luke goes on to record in the following chapter, it all took place on the day of Pentecost. Jesus had also previously said to them; *"Do not think that I have come to abolish the Law or the Prophets; I have not come to abolish them but to fulfil them'.' (Matt 5:17)* For them, 'the Law and the Prophets' would have included God's commandment to gather in Jerusalem for the three major Jewish Festivals. I know there are some Christians who believe we should continue to observe them and this has exercised my mind from time to time. I have reached a conclusion, based largely on what I wrote about the date of Christmas in Chapter Ten. I am content that Tabernacles is fulfilled at Christmas, Passover becomes Easter, and Pentecost is Pentecost, formerly Whitsun. That way I believe we can be faithful to these words of Jesus in Matthew 5:17, provided we do not lose sight of what the original Festivals were all about.

Part of what surprises me in all this, is how quickly it seemed the church concluded Jesus *had* come to abolish the law and the prophets and so set about divorcing itself from the Jewish traditions and teaching. This isolation continues for some people to the present day. On a recent course exploring the Jewish roots of the Christian faith, we heard of one woman who seriously said: *"If I'd known Jesus was a Jew, I'd never have become a Christian."* We have to go back to the beginning, where I believe things started to go awry, such that in time someone should feel able to say something as sad and crass as that.

This gets a little complex but stick with it! Much of the detail is drawn from *'Pentecost is Jewish'* by Danny Litvin, a messianic

Jew and founder of Hope of Israel Ministries.

The inauguration of the Feast of Pentecost is found in Exodus 23:16 where God commands it as a *Feast of Harvest*. The first of the wheat harvest was to be brought to him as a thanksgiving and a reminder that everything we have comes from God and is to be used to his glory. *"The power from on high"* that Jesus said the disciples would receive from the Holy Spirit included a harvest of spiritual gifts that God poured out on the believers present, and desires to do for each subsequent generation. In receiving those gifts, we are to always acknowledge they come from God and are only to be used to his glory and never our own. Later in Exodus 34:22 we are told it is also to be known as the *Feast of Weeks* which in Hebrew is *Shavuot*, the name by which Pentecost is most usually referred to by Jews. Also called a 'week of weeks', the precise day was clearly important and it was to be calculated from the first Sabbath following Passover, that is seven times seven days, making forty nine. As that day would be another Sabbath, a day of rest, Pentecost would be celebrated on the following or fiftieth day. One especially significant thing about all this is that the Jewish feast of Pentecost will always therefore be on a Sunday, the day of Christ's resurrection and inauguration of the New Covenant, that is the Christian Church.

In time, the Feast of Harvest came to include all kinds of other crops. The farmers themselves would take baskets of produce up to Jerusalem, those coming from a distance using dried fruits so they would not spoil on the way. They would arrive before the first day of the Feast and spend the night in the open outside the city. Early in the morning, they would be woken by a call; *"Arise, let us go up to Zion, to the Lord our God!"* The huge procession would be headed up by an ox, its horns covered in gold and on its head an olive wreath. An ox was used because it too had shared in the hard work, along with the farmers. The whole joyful occasion was accompanied by flute players. My own thought at this point is, how much more wonderful that must have been than your average Whitsunday service! I wonder too if our own Harvest Festivals would not greatly increase in meaning if they could be tied in with Pentecost. I realise that in our Spring there would not be much of a harvest to bring, but then again these are meant to be the first fruits. In other words, we are not meant to wait until it's all safely gathered in, but instead bring our thanksgiving to God out of what we have got and believe in faith for what we have yet to receive.

Back in Jerusalem our rejoicing farmers climb the hill toward the Temple and the waiting congregation, on their way singing from Psalms 120 -134, known as the Songs of Ascent. For example Psalm 122 begins; *"Our feet are standing in your gates, O Jerusalem..."* And on reaching the temple entrance, in time for the main act of worship on the first day which began at nine o'clock, they would put their baskets on their shoulders and sing heartily Psalm 150; *"Praise the Lord. Praise God in his sanctuary..."*

Shortly we shall be looking at other Scriptures that were read out, but for now a mention of how important Pentecost remained to the early church; *"Paul had decided to sail past Ephesus to avoid spending time in the province of Asia, for he was in a hurry to reach Jerusalem, if possible by the day of Pentecost." (Acts 20:16)*

These days for the Jew, Pentecost is also celebrated as the time when Moses was given the Law (*Torah*) and in fact this link had already been made by the time of Jesus. In the modern Western world, there is a general suspicion of laws and regulations, even among some Christians who prefer the idea of living in the freedom of the Spirit. So long as we are truly in the Spirit, that's fine, for Jesus also tells us how the Holy Spirit *"will teach us all things" (John 14:26)*. That is indeed how I am sure God intends it to be, provided we are willing to be obedient to what his Spirit teaches. Another, and possibly better meaning for Torah, is instruction and it is surely a fool who believes they can live their life well without instruction. A car driver who has received no instruction is a liability to themselves and others. This added dimension of the Jewish Pentecost fits so well with our Christian celebration of receiving the Holy Spirit, our guide and interpreter of God's word.

Back in the courts of the Temple, the people would be listening to various portions of Scripture, concluding with verses 1-28 of the opening chapter of the book of Ezekiel, which describes an extraordinary manifestation of the glory of God; *"Then there came a voice from above the expanse over their heads as they stood with lowered wings. Above the expanse over their heads was what looked like a throne of sapphire and high above on the throne was a figure like that of a man. I saw that from what appeared to be his waist up he looked like glowing metal, as if full of fire and from there down he looked like fire; and brilliant light surrounded him. Like the appearance of a rainbow on a rainy day, so was the radiance around him. This was the appearance of the likeness of the glory of the Lord. When I saw it I fell face down and I heard the voice of one speaking." (Ezekiel 1: 25-28)*

They would then hear the reader cut to chapter 3 and verse 12; *"Then the Spirit lifted me up and I heard behind me a loud rumbling sound - May the glory of the Lord be praised in his dwelling place!"*

Let me remind you of how Luke recalls this event; *"When the day of Pentecost came, they were all together in one place. Suddenly a sound like the blowing of a violent wind came from heaven and filled the whole house where they were sitting. They saw what seemed to be tongues of fire that separated and came to rest on each of them. All of them were filled with the Holy Spirit and began to speak in other tongues, as the Spirit enabled them." (Acts 2:1-4)* Everyone present heard the sound (verse 6) and gathered around the disciples. Some thought them to be drunk but Peter dismisses this accusation with *"It's only nine in the morning" (verse 15)*, the time at which that prophetic verse from Ezekiel would have just been read out to the thousands who would have been present.

To my mind the tying in of the New Testament account with the Jewish Festival in this way brings a whole new clarity and depth of meaning to what had previously mystified me, not least to the nature and role of the Holy Spirit. And once again it speaks of a wonderful God who acts with such precision and who treasures and fulfils all he has previously given us and would have us see it in the same way. By comparison, the traditional view of the disciples skulking in an upper room, while their fellow Jews are celebrating in the Temple is a sad and impoverished image that I believe is mirrored wherever the Church seeks to resist the Holy Spirit.

POSTSCRIPT

In the concluding chapter of this book, I shall seek to bring together my quest for clarification of the 'tricky bits' with an involvement in Christian healing over a number of years. At Carisbrooke Priory, a key verse for us has often been those words of Jesus; *"Then you will know the truth and the truth will set you free." (John 8:32)* As I understand it, healing to God is all embracing and relevant to individuals, families, nations, races and creation itself. His heart desires reconciliation and restoration of what ever may have been wrongly severed. And it matters not for how many centuries that severing may have prevailed. Part of that restoration he desires is, I believe, between the Church of Christ and its Jewish origins. I am aware this is for some a controversial issue and I believe the apostle Paul gives us more than enough reason why we have no need to keep the letter of the Law of Moses as for example over the issue of circumcision. As he writes to the church in Corinth; *"Circumcision is nothing and uncircumcision is nothing.*

*Keeping God's command is what counts."* *(1 Cor: 7:19)* This whole area was considered in depth at the Council of Jerusalem as recorded in Acts 15. There were dissenting views, not least from those believers who were Pharisees and maintained; *"The Gentiles must be circumcised and required to obey the Law of Moses." (Acts 15: 5)* But under the guidance of the Holy Spirit they were able to conclude and write to the Gentile believers; *"It seemed good to the Holy Spirit and to us not to burden you with anything beyond the following requirements: you are to abstain from food sacrificed to idols, from blood, from the meat of strangled animals and from sexual immorality. You will do well to avoid these things." (Acts 15: 28-29)* My understanding is that such specific guidance was especially for that time and we should look to the Holy Spirit in our own day for what God now requires of us. Without appearing flippant, the call to refrain from blood would rule out black pudding for the conscientious Christian! Quite clearly though our avoidance of sexual immorality is not one to be so lightly dismissed, given that we must still look to God to define in our own day what to him is truly immoral.

As I said earlier, all this is somewhat complex, but as such I believe it shows the value of good scholarship and well considered theology. The whole question of reconnection where appropriate to our Jewish roots is I believe such an important issue, we should give it our careful attention and prayer. Where we discern it is right before God, I believe this reconnection will only lead to a new pouring out of his blessing and power. What better place to start than by placing ourselves alongside the first disciples in the right place on the day of Pentecost ?

## QUESTIONS

1. Where do you think they were on the day of Pentecost?
2. How much do you think it matters?
3. What is your experience of the gift of tongues?
4. What do you understand of the other gifts of the Spirit as for example Paul writes about in 1 Corinthians 12 1-11?

## POEM

I confess to returning to a poem I included in my previous book, *The Holy Caterpillar* as its message sits well with the theme of this Chapter. It explores the nature of *Ruach*, the Hebrew word for both wind, breath and spirit. *'Becalmed'* was written some thirty years ago, while on a house party at Lee Abbey, a Christian Holiday and Conference centre on the North Devon coast.

## BECALMED

Imagine a world
where the wind never blew,
stale air hung heavy,
never renewed;
and no hope of raising up
beautiful cloud,
dying to bless
the dry earth.

Imagine a world
where the trees never stirred,
cornfields stood lifeless,
their windsong unheard,
never to whisper
their language of praise,
never to dance
to their Lord.

Imagine the ocean
bereft of its waves,
never white horses
or thundering spray,
docile and motionless,
starved of its power,
never to change
the Earth's face.

Imagine a heart
where God's breath never blows,
where hatches are battened down,
windows tight closed,
where life is existence
and dreams are denied,
self imposed prisoner
to the day that you die.

# CHAPTER TWELVE
# PULLING IT ALL TOGETHER

*"Now faith is being sure of what we hope for and certain of what we do not see." (Hebrews 11:1)*

I have always loved this verse and return to it many times when facing uncertainty. The writer to the Hebrews goes on to recount many examples of faith in the Old Testament, before beginning to conclude by saying:

*"And what more shall I say? I do not have time to tell about Gideon, Barak, Samson, Jephthah, David, Samuel and the prophets..." (11:32)*

Let me not conclude my epistle by giving the impression I don't have time to deal with a similarly extensive list from Scripture, which in my case prompts me to say *"I don't believe it!"* In all honesty I am happy to stand with the writer of this text and be encouraged by the inspiring examples of faith from a people who had yet to see the Son of God, unlike us Christians. And while some were saved from lions, others were tortured and cut in half, yet not one of them lost their faith in the goodness of God (verses 32-40). I know though I am not alone in finding difficulties with some parts of the Old Testament and realise I have only touched on one of those areas so far. I will shortly have a brief look at a couple of the 'classics', perhaps as a foretaste of another epistle one day.

But first let's consider in general terms how we as Christians might handle the Old Testament. One tragic and misguided reaction is to put it all to one side or worse still seek to disown it, believing somehow that the New Testament is all we need. It had long bothered me that, in many Anglican churches, the set readings at Holy Communion were traditionally an Epistle and Gospel, both of course from the New Testament. In the last century, when Parish Communion became the principal weekly service for most Anglicans, the Old Testament became even more of a closed book for many churchgoers, especially if they seldom read the Bible at home.

Apart from denying ourselves a treasure trove, our ability to know the true Jesus will be seriously impaired and with possibly dire consequences. One of the most extreme examples of this has to be the persecution of the Jews in Germany, a policy that had its roots in the nineteenth century. Theologians had sought to finally divorce the New from the Old Testament and so paved the way for the fallacy of an Aryan Christ and what they believed to be a justification for the attempted destruction of the Jews. This is indeed the extreme, but even today the Church is I believe, impoverished wherever the Old Testament is not honoured, preached and studied. It is even doubtful we should call it the *Old* Testament. Jesus certainly never did. It's all too easy to conclude *'out with old, in with the new'*. I have heard a Messianic believer refer to them as the First and Second Testaments, which I rather like.

It really is a nonsense to imagine one has replaced the other, for Jesus is not only the fulfilment of the Old Testament but for him they were the only Scriptures he knew. Don't forget the New Testament was not written while he was around. It is true he frequently said when teaching; *"It is written (in the Old Testament) but I say to you"* but he clearly had no fundamental problem with the Word of God and far from teaching his disciples to ditch everything that had gone before, he told them specifically he'd not come to abolish it, but fulfil it (Matthew 5:17). I confess I used to think it a bit like the subjects I was taught at school and having done with the exam, I could throw away all the books and notes and get on with what really interested me. If on the other hand you see 'fulfilling' more like someone filling you a glass a water, it would be rather stupid and ungracious to not only refuse to take a sip but also throw it back in their face!

In choosing the title for my last chapter as *'Pulling it all Together'* I hope some of you do not feel I have spent the preceding ones pulling it all apart. Yet one of the valuable things I gained from a liberal training was that when a bone is broken and sets wrongly, the best course of action in the end is to break it again in the hope of resetting it properly. When it comes to matters of faith, this can be quite a distressing experience at the time but one I have come to appreciate. I want to develop this idea a little more but as promised here are some brief thoughts on a couple more tricky bits from the Old Testament.

*"You shall not make for yourself an idol... for I the Lord am a jealous God, punishing the children for the sin of the fathers to the third and fourth generations of those who hate me" (Exodus 20:4-5)* As I wrote in Chapter Five on *'The Man born blind' (John 9)*, I have a serious problem believing in a God who would make a baby blind as punishment for the sins of his parents. I am convinced Jesus did not believe that and did not want his disciples to either. With that conclusion, I found myself then able to revisit this difficult passage from the Ten Commandments. Of course, there is evidence that if a pregnant woman abuses her body through drugs or poor diet, it is more likely her baby will be harmed. Similarly a father who is a habitual criminal is unlikely to be a good role model to his children. But whilst this may be a consequence, I think it too simple to see this purely as punishment for sin, especially when projected to the fourth generation. This verse unfortunately receives a lot of attention in some parts of the healing ministry, seeking to explain someone's present distress as the result, for example, of a great grandfather being a Freemason. I am not suggesting such things may not be important but I would rather

approach this commandment through two crucial points in the text.

First these are those who hate God. I have encountered many who find difficulty in believing in the existence of God, some who hold to strange, irregular beliefs but very few who would admit freely that they *hate* him. Neither do I believe this to be the reaction of a small child being denied by its parents something it desperately wants and shouting at them *"I hate you! I hate you!"* Paradoxically I see such a cry as evidence of a strong bond of love, a love that even encourages such feelings to be expressed. No, this is a deep and entrenched belief that God is somehow untrustworthy and undeserving of our worship, which we consciously choose to give to another deity through an idol. Whilst relatively uncommon, it has to be the most serious breakdown of our relationship with God, who knows well what danger it may bring not only to those so deceived, but also to those for whom they are responsible. As a false belief, it is one we may be driven to instil into our children, who then become responsible for themselves, as I explored in Chapter Six, Jesus' rejection at Nazareth. A loving heavenly Father would be failing in his care if he did not seek to divert us from such a life destroying path.

The second key part of this passage is so often omitted when people quote it, as I confess I deliberately did at the outset. Hands up those who noticed I stopped in mid sentence. The verse actually goes on to say; *"but showing love to a thousand generations of those who love me and keep my commandments." (verse 6)* The difference between three or four and a thousand is not merely numerical. What I understand by this is we have a God who is so much more ready to show mercy and forgiveness than impose punishment. Far from being exclusive to the New Testament this revelation of the true nature of God runs throughout the whole of Scripture. It is not unrelated to our reflections on the three 'lost' parables, where I maintain a true reading of them focuses on the love and diligence of the one who loses, rather than the fickle nature of the one that it lost. Similarly in the Parable of the Sower, we are meant to rejoice in the extravagant generosity of the Sower rather than fret over the frequently unreliable nature of the hearts into which he sows his numerous opportunities. Seeing this commandment in that light, I find it far easier to live with. Like a child who is aware of being the object of great love, they find it far easier to respond with obedience to the one who loves them, knowing they only have their best interest at heart.

And so to my second example from Joshua chapter 7, 'Achan's Sin'. If you're not familiar with it, you may like to read it first, but I warn you it is a distressing story. Achan was a member of the tribe of Judah and wilfully chose to disobey God's command to Israel not to take religious objects as plunder from their enemy at Jericho. His disobedience, we read, provoked God's anger, so that when Israel was next in battle, what should have been an easy victory became a humiliating defeat with many dead. Joshua speaks with God, who explains the problem lies with disobedience. One by one, the tribes and families are eliminated until finally Achan is identified and confesses. The people take him and all his family and all his animals and stone them to death. After this we are told God's anger abated.

I remember the first time I read that story it chilled my heart and at times was tempted to wonder if all this was not something of an over-reaction. Why should those children have to die for the sin of their father? An easy answer is not readily apparent, but what it does impress on me is the need to respect the sovereignty and holiness of God. What I also find reassuring is, whilst shocking, it is a very unusual event. It is far from typical, which leads me to believe it has something to do with the people of God being in a unique situation. They enjoyed a special and intimate relationship with God, especially through Joshua and because they were in a particularly dangerous place. They were so much in it together, that one man's rebellion jeopardised the well being of all. One is reminded of some of the most daring raids during a time of war, when everyone's lives depend on every team member sticking precisely to the plan. I cannot say this causes me to conclude easily *"Oh that's all right then"* but I do believe it a story intended to remind us, never to treat God with contempt nor underestimate the responsibility any head of the house has for their whole family.

But let me draw all this toward a conclusion. I wrote earlier of breaking bones in order to reset them correctly. At the heart of God's great work of redemption is restoration and reconciliation. We may prefer to think this would be nothing but a comfortable, enjoyable experience but at times it may entail first dismantling what has become wrongly and deeply embedded. Discomfort is unavoidable, especially where we may seek to resist the physician's hand. For example, Christian denominations and parties that stubbornly maintain they have a monopoly of truth whilst denigrating others, may in time find their strength wasting away. In the book of Revelation, Jesus speaks of seven churches that are both contemporary to their time and typical in every age. The type demonstrated by the church at Ephesus (Rev.2:1ff) is commended for their hard work and perseverance, but Jesus holds against them the fact that they have lost their first love. This love I believe to be both for God and for their brothers, something that Scripture says is only genuine if synonymous. (1 John 2: 9-11) He calls them to repent, that is to change their way of thinking. If they do not, he will come and remove their lampstand from its place. This curious image should remind all churches that they belong to God and their life and vitality are both given by him and can ultimately be removed by him.

This action of God to break before mending, dismantle before rebuilding runs throughout Scripture, as expressed for example in the prophecy of Ezekiel; *"I the Lord bring down the tall tree and make the low tree grow tall. I dry up the green tree and make the dry tree flourish" (Ezekiel 17: 24)* It is apparent too in Jesus' teaching on the Vine and the Branches (John 15:1-8) where he reveals the work of his Father as the gardener who:

*"Cuts off every branch in me that bears no fruit, while every branch that does bear fruit he prunes so that it will be even more fruitful." (John 15: 2)* On a personal note I cannot help wondering if it is not the case that *"He makes me to lie down in green pastures" (Psalm 23:2)* with among other things the intention of getting me to write a book I might otherwise never have got round to!

I do not believe it is a prerequisite of all healing, but where something is wrongly and firmly established, it may well be. One could think of families crippled by un-forgiveness and infighting, perhaps over generations. Previous overtures of reconciliation by peacemakers have been rejected and it may be only through a tragedy that healing finally comes. Rather than fixating on God as being responsible for not preventing the tragedy, healing comes when it is realised he can turn what was intended for harm to something of far greater good. Joseph declares precisely this to his brothers upon their final reconciliation in Egypt (Genesis 50:20). Though I cannot help thinking if the relationships in that ancient dis-functional family, had not in the first place been so skewed, including Jacob's provocative favouring of one son, there might never have been a need for all the anguish that followed. But then we are human and with that in mind there is no better example of this redemptive principle than the cross of Jesus and all that goes with it.

The night before he dies Jesus keeps Passover, an act of remembrance of God's saving power in rescuing his people from slavery in Egypt. He fulfils Passover in those pivotal words, that have nourished countless millions of Christians ever since; *"Do this in remembrance of me."* Taking the bread and wine as himself, he shares it with all his disciples around the table, including incidentally, Judas Iscariot. And I have long understood this very special 'remembering' to be so much more than a trip down memory lane, a mere nostalgic thumb through the family album. In this context, with Jesus still present today, 'remember' becomes something dynamic, powerful and immediate, nothing less in fact than the antidote to *'dismember'*. The Body of Christ, which is so much more than just the church, has been repeatedly dismembered throughout our blemished history. For that reason I celebrate Holy Communion, the Lord's Supper, the Eucharist, the Mass, (please let us let one another call it what we will), as a major instrument of healing that Jesus has entrusted to us. I know it is not the only instrument and salute those Christians for whom it plays little or no part in their worship. But for me there is something so potentially life changing in this simple and timeless act that Jesus instituted. By it he desires to not only draw us individually closer to God but also **pull us all together**, as he always intended it should be. So forget about *'forgive and forget'* for Goodness' sake let's *forgive and re-member*.

So there we have it, but for a few more words, a final poem and some concluding questions. Thank you for sharing in this journey with me, which I trust you have found helpful, even if at times you may have been unable to agree with me! As I said at the outset these are largely personal responses to those occasions in Scripture when I have been tempted to declare *"I don't believe it!"* I have subtitled the book *Another look at some of the tricky bits of the Bible* and would not presume to say these are the only interpretations. But through making the journey, I believe the Lord has enabled me to deepen my trust in him as the God of all mercy and truth and say with renewed confidence; *"I do believe it!"* I hope and pray this is your experience too.

# REMEMBER

'Take and eat'
I took and ate,
the company
was intimate.
'Take and drink'
I took and drank
and tasted not the tang of wine
nor fed upon the common bread
but given faith
I found instead
unfolding grace
of Life Divine.

QUESTIONS

1. *"For God was pleased to have all his fullness dwell in him, and through him to reconcile all things, whether things on earth or things in heaven, by making peace through his blood shed on the cross." (Colossians 1: 19-20)* Among 'all things' on earth and in heaven, what do you think need reconciling (pulling together) most?

2. What do you make of Achan's Sin in Joshua 7?

3. In what ways should parents seek to instil their beliefs into their children?

4. How important is the Old Testament to you?

5. Is there anything that causes you to say "I don't believe it!" not covered by this book?